The I-Choice
Staying Human in a Digital Age

Fr. Denis Raymond Lemieux

The I-Choice
Staying Human in a Digital Age

Justin Press

The I-Choice
Staying Human in a Digital Age

by Fr. Denis Raymond Lemieux
2888 Dafoe Rd
Combermere ON K0J 1L0
613.756.3713
fatherdenis@gmail.com

is published by

Justin Press
730 Parkdale Avenue
Ottawa, ON K1Y 1J6
613.729.2247
www.justinpress.ca
jdlg@rogers.com

ISBN 978-0-9877805-9-1
Copyright 2013

Legal Deposit, 2013
Library and Archives Canada

Cover Image
Adam and Eve
by Albrecht Dürer
Photo credit: Minneapolis Institute of Arts, MN, USA / The Christina N. and Swan J. Turnblad Memorial Fund / The Bridgeman Art Library

Table of Contents

Chapter One

Digi-Whumped!

Are you on Facebook? Twitter? Got an i-phone? An i-pad? An i-pod? A Kindle? Does your smart phone play podcasts? Can it film movies? Is it Apple or Android? Can you watch webisodes of your favorite show on your Blackberry?

Got a blog? Read blogs? Have you ever blogged on your Blackberry, while updating your Facebook status on your i-phone, then watched the latest viral video on YouTube, after which you tweeted the (viral) links to your followers?

It's good to reflect, as we begin this exploration of the world of technology and the challenges it brings us, that a mere twenty years ago the above paragraphs would have read like a mishmash of nonsense words and phrases. Viral links would have sounded like a sausage-related flu epidemic. I-pods were those things in *Invasion of the Body Snatchers,* an i-pad maybe some kind of louche swinger's hangout (hey baby, wanna come back to my i-pad, wink, wink?).

Podcasts, meanwhile, were a by-product

of shucking peas, and webisodes would have evoked happy memories of those beloved Spiderman cartoons of the 1970s (Spiderman! Spiderman! Does whatever a spider can!). The choice "Apple or Android" would have sounded like some surreal dilemma out of a nightmare (you must decide: I will turn you into a common piece of fruit or a humanoid robot — choose now, or I will kill you!).

Blogs were the places you went to pick cranberries, not blackberries (silly!). To claim you could film movies with your phone would book you an assessment at the local psych ward. Only cult leaders had "followers." Facebook, besides eliciting a lot of blank faces, might suggest some variation on the slam books dear to the hearts of adolescent mean girls everywhere, and Twitter would sound like something only very silly people would do (OK, so not everything has changed in twenty years...).

However, this being the year 2013 and not 1993, all of the above references are familiar and everyday, some of them in fact practically stale from overuse. "I hope this book is not going to be yet another handwringingly-boring lament about the evils of Facebook from some Andy

Rooneyish techno-Luddite!" you might be saying at this point. Or maybe you don't talk like that. Anyhow, don't worry. It won't be.

Oh, technology! How fast it moves and changes! No doubt twenty years from now a whole new vocabulary will have supplanted today's buzz words (a mystical voice is heard coming through the ether from the year 2033: "Are you on Sproing yet? Do you regularly digi-whump your exo-folio?"). Although, given the economic forecasts in the air as I write this book, by 2033, our technological concerns may be less about pixels and more about pickaxes, less "surfing and messaging" and more hunting and gathering. We may all be looking for blackberries for forage, not for e-mail. In that case, this book will be a funny historical artifact of a happier, more prosperous time. Hello, cavemen of the future! Hope you can still read! This book makes great kindling!

Think about it, though: only a hundred years ago, the automobile was just rolling off the Ford assembly line and began shaping our world in radical new ways. Fifty years ago or so, that newfangled invention "television" entered our homes, re-shaping us in an entirely different way, as IQs dropped sharply throughout the land. Thirty years ago, our mode of entertainment was again re-shaped as we suddenly became able to watch our favorite movies whenever we felt like it, and completely failed to pay attention to our surroundings, blasting our cardrums with our tunes while we Walked around, Man.

And it was really only twenty or so years ago that what had been a freakishly science fiction idea — that everyone would one day own a personal computer — suddenly be-came the norm of life, at least in North America, reshaping everything all over again.

Every technological development, in its own way, brought massive cultural change in its wake. This has always been the case, of course: whether it is plastic, pasteurization, the printing press, or papyrus, human inven-tion has continually shaped and re-shaped the human world, more often than not in ways unforeseen and even unwelcomed by the inventors. One small example: Gutenberg was a devout Catholic; that the printing press would become a key driver of the Protestant Reformation would have horrified him.

Today, however, the pace of technologi-cal change is so dizzyingly swift, and the impact of technology on culture is so vast, that it is hard to fathom it fully. Absolutely everything is being affected, and fast: communication skills, reading comprehension, analytical abilities, relationships, social etiquette, modes of entertainment, and education — the very stuff and essence of human life has been and continues to be radically shaped and reshaped by technological development.

What are we to do in the face(book) of all this? Both as human beings, and as Christians (I write this book, as I must, from a Christian perspective, as I will explain shortly), what actually should be our attitude towards this radically shifting world of technology? It seems to me that there are three fundamental points upon which we must agree before we can even begin to address the issue productively.

First, as a missionary people, we have a responsibility to *engage* **the culture** *creatively*. We cannot retreat, even if we might want to, into a low-tech ghetto of our own making, not if we wish to bring the Gospel of Christ to the world. The world exists as it is. Whether or not we like the new technology and its attendant culture, our challenge always is to go there and find a way to communicate Christ there.

Second, as disciples of Christ, we have a duty to make sure that our own cultural formation and identity is in *harmony* **with the path of the Gospel**. The world shaped by technology is fast-paced, and is itself changing quickly, and is quick to shape us according to its own techno-logic, its own agenda, which may or may not be reconcilable with our Christian identity. Our first task as men and women called to the *sequela Christi*, the following of Christ, is to monitor the effect our surrounding culture is having on us, and to be vigilant in preserving our own integrity in the process.

Without this, we cannot be missionaries bringing the Gospel to the digital world, because we will no longer possess the Gospel. *Nemo dabet quod non habet,* the old saying goes: roughly, you can't give what you ain't got.

Finally, as rational creatures made in God's image, Christians, and indeed all men and women of good will, are always challenged to *understand the truth of things and choose the good of things*. No matter who we are or what we believe about ultimate reality, we must never just drift along in a stupor, simply conforming to the dominant cultural paradigms.

I want to reflect in this book on both a human and a Christian approach to technology. My question, to put it very simply, is this: what is technology doing to us, not in itself, but through the accelerated and vast cultural change it is bringing, and what are we supposed to do about it?

I don't have a lot of definitive answers; I think the nature of technology and how quickly it keeps changing will make it difficult if not impossible to arrive at a lot of definitive positions. But I know we need to think, and think carefully, about all of this.

I also know from many conversations I have had during the writing of this book, that many people, perhaps even most people, not only Christians but people from all sorts of ideological and religious positions, have concerns and questions around technological culture which they often struggle to articulate. I hope this book contributes to articulating some of these concerns.

My purpose in this book is not so much to give answers as to start conversations. I want to suggest a basic starting point for those conversations, a fundamental understanding that will allow us to grapple with the many practical decisions we each have to make about the machines we use every day.

This starting point is the absolute imperative to *stay human* **in the midst of the machines**. I think the great danger facing us is a sort of *reductio ad machinam* — a tendency to conform our human expression to the paradigms, formats, modes of the technological devices we use.[1]

This is a terrible diminishment of our being. To put it simply, I am not my Facebook profile. Not all truths can be expressed in 140 characters or less. A hyperlink is not a logical argument. Flame wars and online snark are not the same as critical thinking and dialectic. A Facebook "friend" is not a true friend, except coincidentally. The more our human interactions and human presentation are subordinated to the norms and structures of the technology we use, the more we risk losing a great deal of our full humanity.

---

[1] I am indebted here to Jaron Lanier's book *You are not a Gadget: A Manifesto* (New York: Random House, 2010), which provides a wealth of insight into these questions from the point of view of a software designer cum philosopher.

So this book is about staying human. Now, I realize that in a book subtitled *Staying Human in a Digital Age* the question might well arise, "then why bring Christianity into it? If it is fundamentally a question of preserving our humanity, why not just leave it on that level and write about a human approach to the problem? Why confine your treatment and audience (seemingly) to your own co-religionists?"

Before I can answer that question, I have to address the question lurking behind that question. (Have you ever noticed how often it works that way?) Namely, is there really such a thing *as* humanity? Does human nature exist? This dumps us into deep and perilous philosophical waters that I don't really want to explore at length, but which need to be splashed around in, at least. So everyone relax, fasten your seat belts, put your trays in the upright and locked position. I promise this won't take long.

In the medieval era, the first questions asked upon broaching any topic were the *an sit* and the *quid sit,* roughly translated as 'does it exist?' and 'what is it?' The medievals, so well-known today for their superstitious obscurantism and blind fanatical dogmatism, held the odd belief that one could not productively discuss a subject without first establishing whether it actually existed and what it might be. We've grown beyond that in our enlightened times, and often will spend hours and terabytes in fervent discussions and clamorous disputes without bothering with such boring preliminaries. If the medievals were put in charge of it, the entire Internet would fit onto my laptop.

For example, Thomas Aquinas begins his *Summa Theologiae*, his systematic presentation of the whole science of theology, by first posing the *an sit* of theology — is there such a thing — and then its *quid sit*. Having argued that theology does exist and is the study of God, he immediately proceeds to the *an sit* and *quid sit* of God, and so forth.

At the end of the medieval period, things changed in a dramatic fashion, a change that would affect the whole course of human thought in the West for the ensuing centuries.

The nominalist position advanced by William of Ockham dramatically altered the medieval paradigm, which had its roots both in Greek philosophy and its commitment to rational method, and in Christian faith in a Creator God Who is good and true, and Who desires that human beings should know the truth and goodness of things. Ockham held that it is impossible to really know what a thing is in itself. All we have are our names for things, which are arbitrary.

The reasons for this shift are complex and widely disputed. I suspect it had as much to do with historical events and their psycho-logical-sociological-cultural fallout as anything else. Ockham and his followers wrote in the period of the Black Death, when half of Europe's population died in the hor-rific suffering of the plague. In the subsequent centuries, Muslim invasions were a constant threat to Eastern Europe, eventu-ally reaching as far as the gates of Vienna. Christianity itself was sundered, first in the Great Western Schism of 1378-1417, then in the Protestant Reformation.

While Christianity remained the dominant force in Western Europe for several centu-ries, the medieval vision of a coherent ordered world presided over by a good, lov-ing, all-powerful God was dealt a grievous blow by the calamitous events and sufferings of the fourteenth century and what came af-ter it. In the trauma of early modernity, God seemed to have become inscrutable, arbitrary,

His ways unaccountable, His goodness either in doubt or denied outright. The faltering of faith in this era had far-reaching effects on the mind of Western man.

Without going any further into a historical analysis that is really outside the scope of this book, the trajectory of philosophy since then has largely been in the direction of either a profound agnosticism about the true natures of beings, or an outright denial of "nature" as a meaningful category.

So getting back to the question of humanity and whether or not there is such a thing, some of the most culturally and societally influential philosophy of the past century has been based on an explicit denial of such a thing as "human nature." It is understood in many quarters (the names Sartre, Nietzsche, Comte, and Marx are prominent here, for example, though for widely different reasons) that human freedom demands that we deny an actual binding human nature, with all that that implies: principally, the existence of God and an absolute moral law. At the very least, the construct "human nature" is irrelevant to our choices.

We must be free to create our own nature, our own future, our own world and all it contains. Nothing is "given" — everything is attained by our own efforts and struggles. "We are made, we are not born," as the Parachute Club put it pithily and with a dance beat when I was a wee lad. We can do whatever we want, to put it simply.

So in this post-modern world which would answer either a resounding "No!" to the *an sit* of human nature or an equally definite "We cannot know and do not care!" to the *quid sit,* the very act of writing a book about *Staying Human in a Digital Age* implies that I am taking a dissenting stand here, that I am not a post-modern.

After all, if human beings are defined only as being indefinable and infinitely malleable, then there is nowhere to stay[2] — let technology do what it will with us, and let our human reality be shaped in whatever way we please. Which really means, of course: let the select elite who design and market technological products do what they will with the rest of us, and let them shape

---

[2] Readers who wish to delve into these questions in more depth could find no better guide than Pope Benedict XVI, who has written extensively on these questions. I recommend his books *Christianity and the Crisis of Cultures* and *Values in a Time of Upheaval* (both from Ignatius Press, 2006), and *In the Beginning* (Our Sunday Visitor, 1990).

our reality in whatever way they please. But I'm getting ahead of myself.

I am a Christian. This means that I believe in a Creator God Who made all that is and gives it order and purpose.[3] I believe in a God Who has a plan for creation, and particularly a plan for the human race, a plan that involves in a necessary and vital way the free choice of human beings to enter into it. I believe that God loves us, and that therefore His plan is both good and beautiful, and, furthermore, that it is true.

What I mean by saying that I believe God's plan is good and true is that He does not impose some kind of artificial program from above on His creation. The intentions of God towards us are in a sense intrinsic in the very structure He has given our created reality. How He created us — the structure or nature that He forged in the beginning — and His ultimate purposes towards us are intrinsically related and harmonious, and so salvation or redemption comes to us as

---

[3] This belief in God as Creator must be sharply distinguished today from belief in *Genesis* 1 as a scientific or historical account of the process of creation. I believe in *Genesis*, but as a theological statement about the origin, goodness, and purpose of creation, not as a quasi-scientific description of how God did it.

something that fulfills the deepest desires of our hearts.

I believe as a Christian that God's plan for humanity is revealed in and through Jesus Christ. I believe, then, that questions of humanity and staying human cannot be understood or discussed at any length (at least not by me!) without reference to the Christ-centered and God-given nature of it all. I will have more to say about all of this in a later chapter.

Does this mean that this book has nothing to offer the non-Christian reader? I hope not. As I intend to develop throughout the book, a great deal about this "human nature" that I am concerned to defend and which I believe should guide our use of technology can be known through reason and experience. Most of my observations about what it means to be human do not spring in their origin from Divine Revelation, even though I believe that the full truth of humanity can only be found there.

I intend this book to be part of a broad conversation across the whole of contemporary society about technology and humanity. Surely the Christian voice should or at least can be part of this necessary conversation, as should the Muslim, Jewish, Hindu, Buddhist, Confucian, and animist voices, along with the voices of the non-religious. We all are united in our common need to face and make sense of the world that technology is fashioning around us. No person of good will should be excluded from the dialogue.

I will not spend much time talking about specific uses of technology, and how it can be used explicitly for good or evil ends. The internet can be used to preach the Gospel, to mobilize large groups of people quickly in a united effort, make information of all sorts instantly available worldwide, and generally send beauty and truth of all kinds into the world. It can also be used to disseminate pornography, bigotry, slander, hate mongering, gossip, and nonsense. All of these are fairly obvious good or evil uses of technology. At the very least, their relative goodness or lack thereof stems from their content, not from the technology used in their delivery. Gossip is gossip, whether it's delivered over the back fence or a Twitter feed.

I want to reflect instead on technology itself — how do the machines themselves and the way in which they work affect us? What kind of world do we inhabit as we spend more and more of our time on them? How are our culture and our very selves being shaped by technology? And what specific challenges does this pose for humanity in the year 2013?

Technology is neither good nor bad in itself, I would argue — it is just is what it is. But the very speed of technological change is negative in one sense: the urgent pace and constantly changing face of the techno-world require us, or at least seem to require us, to constantly run to keep up. We have no time to think, to consider, to review, to step back and look at the machines we use and the effects they are having on us.

It is hard for us to pause and ask the questions that every free human being must be able to ask about virtually everything presented to them, namely: What is this? Do I want this? Is it good? Think of this book as, in a sense, a "pause button", inviting you to stop briefly and explore the issues at stake here.

I want to make it clear from the outset that I am not anti-technology. I wrote this book on a laptop, I am on Facebook, and I have a blog.[4] I am also not especially pro-

---

[4] "Life With a German Shepherd", at frdenis.blogspot.com, if you're interested!

technology, although I will admit to being more than a little fascinated by all the bells, whistles and shiny buttons it specializes in. If not a full-fledged "out and proud" computer nerd, I am well in touch with my inner geek who yearns to be at play in the binary fields of the Lord and who (truth be told) really just wants an i-pad all his own.

I am neither pro- nor anti-technology. **What I am is *pro-humanity*.** My bottom line is this: technology is good if it serves humanity in the fullest sense of the word; technology is bad, or at least bad for you, if it diminishes your humanity in any way. This is going to be the overarching theme and structure of this book.

What does it mean to be human? What are the qualities and characteristics of a fully human life? Where is the explosion of information technology most radically affecting this human life, and how are we to respond?

These are the questions I will be raising. As I have said, my hope is not to provide ready-made easy answers, but to provoke reflection and debate. I am convinced that both of these activities — reflection and debate — represent some of our most precious and valuable human capacities, capacities which are in my view imperiled by the impact of technology. Reflection requires silence and attentiveness; debate requires critical thinking skills; the Internet, frankly, encourages neither. If this book stimulates either, even just a little bit, that alone will help us make strides towards a more fully human integration of technology into our world.

Chapter Two

Servant and Master

So where do we begin this task of a full human integration of technology? What is the essential human reality that we need to lay hold of so as to preserve it? It seems futile to talk about "staying human," even if we grant the legitimacy of this desire, if we have no meaningful concept of what a human being is.

There are many possible legitimate starting points to answering this question. The relational nature of human life is crucial, along with the familial and political dimensions it gives rise to (see Chapter Seven); the creative element is also important (*homo faber* — man the maker, which I will discuss in Chapter Eight).

But I want to begin with two related aspects of our humanity which, since the time of the ancient Greeks, have been understood as essential, two elements in us that make us the kind of creatures that we are. In Christian terms, we would put it that every human being is endowed with two faculties that are given to us by God.

As far as we know, since E.T. has not yet shown up either to phone home or blow up the White House (depending on what mood he/she/it is in), these faculties distinguish us from the rest of material creation. They are thus essential to our humanity — the essential difference between the animals and us. As I will show, they are equally essential to the human pursuit of our divinely ordered destiny.

These faculties, which are deeply interwoven, are **intellect and rational will**. Simply put, we are made to *know the truth* of things and to *freely pursue the known good* of things.

Once upon a (medieval) time, this would have passed as an obvious truism. Today, it is anything but. All this "truth and goodness" business is deeply controverted in the world today, and so we have to make a short digression here to at least explain what we mean by these words.

Relativism is the air we breathe in the post-modern world. There is no Truth, we are told, only my truth, your truth, his truth, her truth. And the same holds for goodness — there is no goodness per se, only what each determines to be good for him-or-herself.

This position, which is so widespread as to be virtually conventional wisdom today, is deeply muddleheaded and incoherent. There is no truth; and this is advanced as a true statement. Or, we cannot know the truth; yet we claim to know this. Everyone must decide for himself what is good and evil; you are committing a great evil if you disagree with that proposition. At every step, relativism, advanced as an actual philosophical stance, contradicts itself.[5] Of course, more often than not, it is not really held as an explicit philosophy, but as a set of fuzzy slogans and a vague desire to be tolerant and nice, along with a not so nice or vague desire to make everyone who disagrees with you or offends you shut up.

We have to reclaim the idea of truth — that there is truth available to us about reality. We have the faculty of intellect, and it is made to know the truth. But what does that mean? What is truth, anyhow, as Pontius Pilate asked in somewhat different circumstances?

Truth, says Thomas Aquinas, is "the adequation

---

[5] It would be outside the scope of this book to go into a full discussion of relativism here. Besides the previously cited works of Pope Benedict, my own thoughts on the subject can be found in "Breathing the Post-Modern Air," in *Restoration,* October 2011, available at www.madonnahouse.org.

of the intellect to the object."[6] This rather technical definition is actually not that hard to understand. At every moment, we are bombarded with sensory data — our eyes, ears, noses, skin take in information about their immediate surroundings. The traditional Aristotelian-Thomistic theory of knowledge is that our intellects have the capacity to abstract from this sensory data the actual in-itself reality of the object that is the source of this sensory data. In other words, "truth" means that reality is presenting itself to our minds through our senses in such a way that our minds can take it in and make a home for it, so to speak. There is room in our mind for all of reality. There is a correspondence between the way our minds work and the way things really are; hence, this theory of knowledge is often called the "correspondence theory".

To put it a bit poetically, every being that presents itself to us is continually telling us its name, and if we are attentive and thoughtful, the true name of each being can live in our minds. An entire philosophy of communion and harmony emerges from this traditional

---

[6] *Quaestiones Disputatae: Volume 1: De Veritate*, (Rome: Marietti, 1949)

understanding of the mind. We are not strangers and aliens floating around in a hostile cosmos made up of nonsensical fragments. Our task is not to impose our own ideas, our own "truth," whatever that means (generally it means, "whatever I want"), onto these obdurate mute fragments.

First, **we are to contemplate, receive, take in reality, to such an extent that we can then reflect, analyze, and reason correctly about it**. In the Catholic intellectual tradition, it has always been understood that this analytical reasoning process takes us far beyond the immediate sensory objects and their own natures. The intellect beginning from sensory data can reason its way towards all sorts of invisible realities: God, the soul, the moral law. And so, from this intellectual process of reflection we can obtain a true knowledge of reality so that we can determine how to move and live in such a way as to achieve the good: what will make us happy.

And this leads us directly to the second great faculty essential to our humanity, namely our *free will*. The intellect is essentially receptive and contemplative in its first movement, taking in reality in the act of comprehension; the will in its movement is essentially acting and initiatory. **Will is that by which, in harmony with the intellect, we determine what is the good thing to do in order to attain our proper end, and spur ourselves into action towards achieving that good.**

There is a lot to be said about the will, and, indeed, it is one of the most complex and somewhat mysterious elements of our humanity. By the intellect we determine (note, not invent) the good, but it is our will by which we move towards that good. By our intellect, we examine the different means to attain a specific end, but it is our will that chooses and spurs us into action towards those means.

Without getting into the truly complex philosophical and psychological issues around the will, perhaps for this study it is worth mentioning the harmony that underlies the action of intellect and will, and their underlying unity with both the world in its ordered state and God Who is the author of this order.

In the post-modern view, this harmonious picture of unity and order is denied. The will wants what it wants, and the intellect (if allowed in at all) has only one function, which is to carry out the will's imperious commands. Intellect in this view becomes no more significant than the bear's claws or the crocodile's jaws; it is a tool to get you what you want. We are merely clever beasts, as a bear or a lion is a strong beast. God (if His existence is acknowledged) is either passive and irrelevant or, if active, He is our enemy, thwarting us at every step, and the world is an anomic jungle, a Hobbesian struggle for domination where each is pitted against each.

In the classical and medieval view, God is not the enemy, but the ultimate end of our striving, the fulfillment of all desires, as Ralph Martin put it recently in his book of that title. God *is* the Good towards which we are striving. The world is that field where we come to know what is good, through the exercise of our intellect informed by our senses, and to love that good and direct our actions towards it, so that with God's grace we ascend to our final End, to Ultimate Good. Intellect and will are finely woven together in a complex relationship, intellect taking in reality, will shaping and shaped by that process, and moving out in truth towards the good the intellect has apprehended, God giving light and help at every turn.

It has been necessary to go on at some length here, precisely because we are so deeply confused and confounded in this most vital and central area of our humanity. To some degree, this confusion has always been present; as our intellects and wills have been darkened and weakened by original sin, and our trust in God and love for the world deeply compromised by the same.

Today, though, this confusion has been raised to new heights, and profoundly impedes our ability to live peacefully and purposefully in the world. If truth and goodness are not attainable by our intellects, if freedom is a meaningless cipher, not being pointed towards any good end, if God is silent and distant or null and void, if the world is a jungle or cesspool or desert or dung heap or whatever other nasty image you choose to employ — if all of that is the case, then human happiness is at best a fleeting grab at passing pleasure, at worst a mocking chimera.

I am a Christian. I hold that we have intellect and will, and that these essential faculties of our humanity root us in reality and point us towards the good, the happiness for which our Creator has made us.

This first and central expression of what it means to be human is extremely relevant in regard to the world of information technology. As I said in the previous chapter, I truly am not pro- or anti-technology, but I do have deep concerns about it precisely here, in relation to our use of our intellect and will.

To put it in a simple, obvious way, if we arc to usc tcchnology in a human way, then we have to *think* about it, to deliberate and be careful in our choices. Am I going to use this device or not, buy it or not? How am I to use it?

The trouble here is that so much of these discussions — what technology is, how and when it is to be used — is being driven if not outright controlled by the very people who make and sell high tech equipment and software.

That's a problem, isn't it? Bill Gates, Mark Zuckerburg, the clever crowd at Google, Jeff Bezos, whoever's doing the job of Steve Jobs (RIP) at Apple, etc., are the ones who determine to a large extent how we talk about all this stuff. That being the case, it turns out (surprise!) that you in fact "need" to buy an i-phone, or i-pad, or

Kindle! You "need" the latest Windows platform, and a new laptop every two years. You "need" to have an i-pod that can hold 100,000 songs. You "need" to be on Facebook.

I suggest that this high-pressure, hard-sell world of technology can indeed impinge on our intellects and will. Fear tactics and peer pressure make us feel as if we really do need to get with the program no matter what. The techno-rapture is taking all the cyber-saved up into the cloud computer (the Spirit in the Skynet) — don't be left behind! All your friends are on Facebook or whatever will be the next big social media network — well, come on — you do want friends, don't you? What are you, a hermit or something? Information media run on a 24-7 globalized cycle fuelled by an endless stream of Twitter feeds and blog posts — either get ahead of the story or become the story! Tweet or be twitted, in short.

Peer pressure, fear tactics, and the hard sell are hardly unique to the world of technology, of course. Peer pressure has been employed ever since Eve handed Adam the apple ("c'mon, Adam — just one bite!

What's the matter — you chicken?"). Noah probably used fear tactics to get his more reluctant children on the ark ("*Après moi, le deluge,*" he said, justifiably, although probably not in French). The hard sell was no doubt used to sell time shares in the Tower of Babel (and some of the wording in the fine print of the contract was *especially* hard to understand — good grief, what language is this written in…oh, yeah…).

So what's the problem? Besides the fact that none of those hard-sell tactics are ever good, but are always manipulative, the particular problem here is the degree to which information technology is indisputably shaping and re-shaping our world and ourselves constantly in dramatic, drastic ways . . . and there's no real discussion going on. There doesn't seem to be any real broadly based forum for raising concerns.

Oh, people like me are writing books and articles, and a few people still have the synapses available to read them (Hello reader! Nice to see ya! Next time bring a friend!), but what about everybody else? What about all these young and not-so-young people who don't read books anymore, but get all their written word information from the short and snappy world of Wikipedia, status updates, and blogs? [7] What input or thoughtful reflection are they getting about all these matters? It seems to me that, for society at large, the whole discussion around technology is largely driven by people who have economic interests in getting you to buy, buy, buy whatever the newest thing is.

So the first point in the human use of technology is that we need to use it like human beings. In other words, we have to think about it. We have to be the one choosing. We have to be free about our choice.

So, you can say, "You know, I really don't want to be on Facebook — it's a stupid waste of time!" Or, equally, "I do want to be on Facebook — it helps me to stay in touch with people." Or, "I don't want an i-pod — I find it makes me a bit too self-absorbed," or on the other hand, "I want an i-pod — it gives me easy access to so many things I treasure."

The key thing, as far as I can see, is not

---

[7] See Nicholas Carr, *The Shallows: How the Internet Is Changing Our Brains,* (New York: WW Norton, 2010). Also, Mark Bauerlein, *The Dumbest Generation: How the Digital Age Stupefies Young Americans and Jeopardizes Our Future,* (New York: Penguin, 2009).

the actual decision we make, but that we are the ones thinking it through and deciding. We must not allow ourselves to be manipulated or pressured to go along with what everyone else is doing.

Of course, it's understood that on the job things are different — we all have to work with the technology of our trade. As I have said, I wrote this book on a laptop and e-mailed the manuscript to my publisher — quill and ink were not involved in the process. But, away from your job (hoping you have one!) and its proper demands, **it is utterly necessary to be free and sovereign in the choices you make**.

There is a very basic issue of human dignity at stake here. Don't allow yourself to be e-bullied. Don't be an i-patsy, a cyber-wuss. As the saying goes these days, but I mean this in its deepest sense, "Man up!"

Of course, there's more to being a "man" than just being rational and free. These are necessary capacities that allow us to negotiate our way through this world towards the world to come, in truth and in goodness. But then questions are raised . . . what is the truth of things? What is the true good for human beings?

We have intellect and will, but for what? What are they supposed to be aimed towards? These ultimate big questions go beyond the discussion of technology, which is the subject of this book, but cannot be wholly ignored. We cannot fully understand any specific area of human striving without having some sense of the big picture, of how it all fits into the deeper questions of ultimate purpose and meaning. We can know all the techniques of cooking, haberdashery, and bicycle repair, but a true understanding of any of them requires at least some sense of how food, clothing, and locomotion serve us in attaining our final goal. Technical prowess is ultimately worthless without wisdom, without knowing what it's all for.

The next chapter will present a summary of the Christian answers to these deep questions — a sort of short catechism of the faith. The subsequent chapters, which will look at some basic human experiences and needs affected by the technological revolution, will discuss these in light of the ultimate horizon of our lives. If you are reading this book, and are not a Christian or are unsure, then I invite you to reflect on your own view of ultimate meaning and horizon, and how this is to inform your use of technology.

But at this point of our exploration, the bottom line is this: **technology must be our servant, not our master**. Each one of us in our sovereign freedom must order this servant to carry out our intentions, intentions that we have devised from the operation of our own intellects and our own perception of the good we are seeking. We must never allow our intentions to be shaped by the technology.

In summary, Man is the master of the machine.

Chapter Three

The Big Picture

I have always cherished the story of the college freshman who was taking a course on Comparative Religion. Week after week, she would come home to her parents and tell them with great enthusiasm about all the exciting, exotic religions of the world and their fascinating beliefs and practices.

Finally, her father said to her, "Well, have you gotten yet to the one where God became everything we are so that we could become what God is?"

She was intrigued and answered him, "No, which one is that?"

Oh yeah, Christianity. It reminds me of one of my brother priests in Madonna House. He grew up in the foothills of the Rocky Mountains. One time, he showed me a post card of a majestic, stunningly beautiful, snow-capped mountain rising up out of the plain. At the very bottom of the card was a teeny little house, barely noticeable against the enormous beauty. Pointing at it, he said, "That's the house I grew up in."

In fact, that's the house most of us grew up in. This vast mountain, this breathtakingly beautiful immense fact in our back yard — Christianity. Whether we believe it or not, love it or hate it or even (rarely) are indifferent to it, it's such a huge reality, all-pervasive in every facet of our culture, that we barely notice what a strange and fantastical thing it is.

In this chapter, I can do no more than provide a basic sketch of the Christian religion, writing (as I must) from a Roman Catholic perspective. There is something about Christianity that inspires literary output; we have been an incurably wordy bunch, from Pentecost Sunday on. Therefore, those wanting a fuller presentation of Christianity than is offered here will find no shortage of material. Nor will it be possible for this briefest of brief sketches to anticipate and answer all the possible objections thrown up against the faith — again there is no shortage of controversial or apologetical works available to those who wish to explore Christianity from that angle. Take it for granted that I am aware that almost every sentence of this chapter has been argued over, disputed about, vehemently disagreed with, etc., etc. I have neither time nor space in this book to go into all that.

The purpose of this chapter existing in a book about technology and our human use of it is to ground the discussion in the subsequent chapters in the fundamental vision of reality that flows from the Christian proclamation. Hence, while I will try to be as comprehensive as possible while remaining as concise as possible, some of the emphases in what follows will reflect the specific challenges and questions the rest of the book will discuss more fully. With that, let us begin.

God

God is love (1 *John* 4:8). This is the proper starting point. Now, the statement that "God is love" can seem sentimental or vague, a bit uncertain in meaning, perhaps. But it is actually the heart of the matter for us.

By saying God is love, we are saying that God is, in His very self, a movement towards the good of the other. Love seeks the good of the beloved; God *is* Love, and, therefore, one way of describing God would be as a sort of benevolent energy at the heart of the world.

Of course, as soon as the word "energy"

is mentioned, red flags rightly go up. But this energy that is God is not some kind of New Age vagueness: He is love, and therefore *personal*. He is revealed to us throughout the Jewish and Christian Scriptures as a *person,* as One Who from the beginning is engaged with us in a passionate love affair. He is not merely some free-floating cloud of benevolent divine power.

In fact, with Jesus and the fullness of the Christian revelation we discover that this God is a Trinity of Persons, while remaining One God. This is difficult to understand, to say the least. Indeed, we only know about this because Jesus revealed it to us when He revealed Himself as Son of the Father who sends the Spirit to complete His work, all the while identifying Himself and His Father with the One God Who revealed Himself to the fathers, to Moses, to the prophets.

Briefly, to shed what feeble light I can on this dogma of the Trinity, God the Father from all eternity "begets" the Son, pouring out His whole Divine being in this eternal gift of life and love; God the Son eternally receives this gift from the Father and returns it, giving all His love and life to the Father in an eternal act of love; this eternal and infinite gift of love and life between Father and Son is so total that from it proceeds a third Person, God the Spirit, Who is this very movement of eternal love from Father to Son and back again.

Without trying to penetrate the mystery of the Trinity (which is anyhow impossible to do), what the doctrine of the Trinity implies is that this love-which-is-God is not only a love for everything that is not God, i.e., for all His creatures, but rather lies at the very heart of the Godhead. In other words, God *is* relationship, communion-in-Himself. God is, in a manner that is utterly beyond our comprehension, a communion of love, and, since God is by definition the ultimate central Reality of all reality, that from which and to which everything else flows, then relationship, communion, love is at the very heart of everything. This is the key to everything that follows.

Creation-Man-Sin

God in His perfect divine life is not needy or lonely, as some have said. The doctrine of the Trinity establishes that. Already, in God, there is a fullness of relationship, of gift, of life and love that beggars our imagination, but which we hope to spend eternity learning about. So, if He had no need for it, why did He create the universe? Why did He make us?

It is because He is good that He did this. It is the nature of goodness to communicate itself to others. "The good is self-diffusive" is the formulation that comes to us from our medieval teachers. So God, having totally shared Himself within Himself, if we can put it that way, desires to extend the communion, the relationship, to what is not God. In other words, this personal God creates non-divine persons that He can invite into communion with Himself.

Andrei Rublev's icon of the Trinity expresses this in a clear, beautiful way. This icon depicts the event of *Genesis* 18:1-15, where Abraham is mysteriously visited by three visitors who are somehow identified as "YHWH," to whom he offers a meal. These mysterious three are seen by the fathers of the Church as a sort of mystical foreshadowing of the Trinity. In Rublev's icon, the three are at the table sharing the meal. Each is inclined towards the others, but the composition of the three opens up — there is not only room at the table for a fourth, but the three are so arranged as to draw the one viewing the icon towards that open space.

This is the heart of the matter for the theology of creation. In creating the universe, and particularly in His creation of rational spiritual persons, God has "opened up" a space at the table for us, invited us in, to share and participate in His own goodness and life. This is what being made in "God's image and likeness" is all about, and what Adam's rapture at seeing Eve who is "bone of his bone, flesh of his flesh" is all about. The whole overflowing goodness of creation and its human dimension reveals that God Who is love made us to be love; God Who is communion created us for no other reason than to be in communion with Him and each other.

Clearly, this did not come off without a hitch. This communion was broken; how, when and where we do not really know. The first three chapters of *Genesis* are deeply true, but they are not history in the normal sense of the word. Our communion with God is a communion in obedience. Unlike the Persons of the Trinity Who are equally God in their divine relations, we are not God's equals. We receive existence from Him and are held in existence by Him. He is the shaper, the fashioner, the author, and hence the authority. The radical receptivity which is at the heart of our creaturely existence necessarily means that we owe obedience to Him, and our communion with Him in truth and with one another is lived in that obedience.

Somehow, we broke that obedience, defied that authority, spurned the gift of love and communion He had given us. And so, the whole tragic dimension of human life came into being: alienation, misunderstanding, jealousy, hatred, violence, death. God made us to be above the angels; we made ourselves lower than the beasts.

Sacred History

God, however, is bigger than we are, and smarter too, and His ultimate designs are not frustrated by human sin. The Hebrew Scriptures show us, in summary, God's work to re-establish the relationship, to rebuild the communion with His creature man. He does this by selecting one small tribe out of all the tribes and nations on earth. He gradually reveals to them what He needs them to know: that He has chosen them to be His very own people; that He has given them a land, a law, and a temple in which they are to worship

Him, in which they are to learn who He is and how to live in communion with Him. They fail Him repeatedly, but He continually refashions the relationship, rebuilds the communion. In this, they begin to see more clearly His awesome faithfulness and love.

The sacred history of Israel is a messy one. God has to meet His people where they are to begin with, and the reality of human sin had taken them very far indeed from where He wanted them to be. Many of the most difficult and baffling passages in the Old Testament reflect that tension, that distance: the passages filled with violence and slaughter and grotesque events.

We have always understood God's self-revelation to be progressive and only fully comprehensible in the coming of Jesus Christ. All of the Old Testament is read through the lens of the full revelation of Christ, and given a new and true meaning consonant with this full revelation.

All of the sacred history of Israel occurs fully embedded in the real history of the ancient world, its wars and empires, and all this ancient history is taken up into and made part of the revelation of God. In other words, in our sacred history we are not living in the land of myths, but rather in the Fertile Crescent from the years (roughly) 1000 BC — 100 AD, the world of Egypt, Assyria, Babylon, Persia, Greece, and Rome. This also is key to the big picture: our God is not a fairy tale or a myth; He acts in history and geography, time and space, to attain His purposes.

By the end of the Old Testament era, the Jewish people had lived under a succession of foreign empires for centuries, and had come to the realization that their little kingdom would never be restored by any human political process. And so they were waiting for God to reveal Himself in an entirely new way, to bring about a new state of affairs by a new and entirely divine outpouring of power. They looked for the heavens to open for a new action and revelation of God, and this is the meaning both of the word *apocalypse* and its expression in literature and life in this time.

Jesus Christ

"And the Word became flesh and dwelt among us..." This revelation, this apocalypse of God came in a way that was wholly unexpected. There is very little in the Jewish

Scriptures that could prepare the Jews for this entirely new action of God, which indeed can only be described as a new creation.

God the Son through Whom all things were made became a human being. God Who is infinite "bound" Himself to a finite human nature: body and soul, time and place. God Who could not suffer made Himself able to suffer in His human nature. God Who is Life itself made Himself able to experience death by uniting Himself to mortal flesh.

This, if it is true (which it is, I believe with all my heart!), is the most extraordinary thing ever to happen, that will ever happen this side of the Second Coming, that ever could happen. Two thousand years of proclamation, of formulation, of theology, and of lived experience of its implications in Christian life have not dimmed its luster, its splendour, its awesome power. The all-powerful God became a baby, a little boy, a youth, a young man, a grown man, a suffering man, a dying man, a corpse.

Why? Because God is love. And He made us to be in communion with Him. And our persistent refusal of that communion had to be overcome. So, without committing sin Himself, which for God is a metaphysical impossibility, He jumped over the barrier between creature and Creator and joined us in our exile from Him. There is just no other story in the world like this — isn't it a shame that familiarity with it has so often made us so indifferent to it?

One of my secret hopes around the growing secularization of our society is that eventually people will be so ignorant of Christianity that some will come to hear this story told to them as a brand new experience, something they really have never heard of before, and so recover a sense of its sacred awe. God became a man! Really?? Come, let us adore Him!

So what did this Jesus do? Briefly, He recapitulated everything God had revealed of Himself in the Hebrew Scriptures and applied it to Himself in a new and startling way. He healed and gave life. He overcame evil spirits and forgave sins. He gave a law with authority. He proclaimed a new kingdom. He rebuked the sins of His people, but His emphasis was always on mercy. He called disciples to follow Him, and appointed twelve to become the foundation of the "New Israel," His Church.

And then He died. The death of Jesus on

the Cross and exactly how it makes a difference to our relationship with God is a surprisingly difficult one in theology. Over the centuries, many different ways of explaining it have been proposed; the Church itself has blessed these theories, but officially endorsed none of them. We simply stay with the Biblical teaching: Jesus died in obedience to His Father's will, this death in some fashion wins us the forgiveness of our sins and opens heaven to us, and is in some fashion parallel to the sacrifices offered in the Jewish temple, the difference being that it is a perfect sacrifice with power to cover the sins of the whole human race forever with its effectiveness. His death saves us, and so Jesus is the Savior of the world.

As I say, different explanations have been offered for this deeply mysterious reality at the heart of the Christian faith. Perhaps all of them are true; perhaps the full explanation of how this God-become-man dying on a cross changed everything for all people forever is really beyond our limited human capacity to understand.

Here is my own best way of understanding it: God is life and being itself, their source and the One who most fully possesses, or rather IS, these things. Our own life and existence flow solely and absolutely from our communion with Him, a communion (as I have already said) that is lived out by our obedience to His will. So disobedience (sin), which breaks this communion, removes us from the source of life and being. Hence, the wages of sin are death, not essentially because God punishes us for our sins by striking us dead, but because sin "unplugs" us, if you will, from the only life-source there is.

So dissolution and death are the ultimate expression of sin and of our breaking the communion with God which is our sole *raison d'être*. Death is the place of no-God, no-life, no-goodness, no-love. The place of negation. And so, God becoming man in Jesus freely chooses out of love for us to plunge into this ultimate place of negation and plants there, I suggest, in some fashion that we cannot fully grasp, His own absolute yes — the yes of the sinless man to God and the yes of God to human beings that is His act of supreme mercy towards us.

And so at the very furthest remove, the ultimate distance we human beings can attain from God, in the very pit of death and nothingness and all that is most opposed to God, we are met by . . . God. Life meets us precisely where there is no life, and so death is defeated and robbed of its power.

This opens for us a new chapter in the human story, a new beginning, creates hope for us. Heaven is open, because Christ has harrowed Hell, and we do not have to go there. Death is not the end, and the Resurrection of Christ is the radiant sign of that victory which is our hope and our joy even now, as we labor in a world still marked by sin and death in so many grievous ways.

Church

This new story, then, is the life of the Church, which is the life of Christ being lived out in the body of believers who are joined to Him by grace. The events of 2000 years ago are eternal events, events done by God, fundamentally, and hence transcending strict categories of time and space and history, but for us human beings who live in time, space, and history, they seem like events of the distant past. We need something concrete, some visible reality where we can encounter Christ and know ourselves to be part of this new story He has fashioned at the heart of the old human story.

This is the work of the Spirit, fundamentally: to extend the story, the life, the presence, the action, the mission of Christ to all men and women of all times and places, and to bring us together into a body, a family, a new Israel, the beginning of the kingdom of God configured to and oriented around our King and God, Jesus the Christ. And this work of the Spirit is the creation and sustaining in life of the Church.

The Spirit does His work through the external realities of Church — institutional structures, development of doctrine, liturgical rituals, cultural expressions of faith — and through His mysterious action in the hearts of each believer, purifying, sanctifying, empowering each to love and live as Christ loved and lived.

With the introduction of the Church into the Christian "big picture," we meet a key concept, namely **the *sacramental* character of reality**. The big picture is filled with cosmic, eternal, and deeply mysterious events, movements, beings. Sacramentality means that all of this immense reality of God and man and salvation is expressed for us in ways accessible to our tiny little human capacities.

God washes us clean, makes us a new creation, fills us with His Spirit, initiates us into the kingdom — big realities; water flows over the head of a baby and the simple words of baptism are spoken. God fills us with His Spirit to strengthen and enlighten us in our growth towards sanctity; oil is smeared on the forehead; God continually gives His whole self to us to draw us into His own triune life and make it our life; bread and wine become Christ's body and blood to be our spiritual food and drink.

Besides the seven Sacraments that are the assured and certain channels of Christ's grace in the life of the Church, the broader principle of sacramentality applies to everything in the Christian big picture. The Church itself is a sacrament, making visible the invisible reality of the communion of love the human race is meant to be, which flows out of our being reconciled to God.

The whole Marian dimension of Christianity is sacramental: God fashioned a human being who would perfectly live and reveal the path of redeemed humanity in her created being, and who would stand with and for all of us as a helper and guide, as our spiritual mother in our own journey of redemption.

At every turn in Catholic Christianity, we are met by a sacramental approach; the use of art and music, incense and linens and candles revealing the beauty of worship; the proliferation of religious communities and monasteries making visible the immense creativity of God opening up a host of different ways to be Christian in the world; the Church's sexual ethics which insist that human sexual expression has been given a sacramental meaning by God, embodying the mystery of His life-giving love and hence being morally good only between a married couple who are open to life and procreation; the call to Christian love and service, which makes visible the love of God for the world through the love of men and women for one another and especially for the poor and afflicted.

All of reality for us now points to another reality. Every particle of creation truly has a sacramental quality. The beauty of creation, the natural genius and creativity of men and women, the delightful innocence and simplicity of children, all the textures and contours of relationships, families, friendships: the whole human experience points to another reality, to this mystery of God, His superabundant goodness, His overflowing charity, His mercy and love.

Even the painful realities, whether the humiliating failures of Christians both clerical and lay to manifest any kind of love in their lives, or all the deep sufferings and evils that afflict the world in ways all too familiar to us — even these point to one further deep truth that is essential to the Christian big picture. Namely, we are not at the final stage yct. The last chapter of the world has yet to be written; the story has not yet been resolved in an adequate, satisfying way.

The last element of the Christian big picture is that we are headed towards something different and new. The way things are now is not the way they will always be. There is a Second Coming of Christ, a final judgment, an ultimate resolution of all the evils and injustices of the world, an ultimate and permanent healing of all wounds, a final victory of God in which all who desire it will be caught up into a communion, a unity, an exchange of love and life that will bear us all into the very heart of the Trinity where we will live and love and rejoice forever.

THE BIG PICTURE

Well, that's the Christian big picture — the truth and goodness that our lives are meant to be directed towards at all times. At least, that's the best job I can do in this small space to describe it! In light of where I'm going in this book on technology and the issues it raises for humanity, I want to highlight some of the fundamental themes I've touched upon in this chapter that are relevant to what will follow.

First, that it is all about *relationship,* our love for God and one another.

Second, that this relationship is all about *obedience,* surrender to the will of God, which is a will of perfect love and goodness towards us.

Third, that this relationship of obedience gives life a deeply *interior* dimension — as human beings we are called to live out of our deep hearts from which we can give and receive love.

Fourth, that at the same time this deeply interior relationship with God has an outward *sacramental* expression; it is to be concretized, made visible and sensible in a wide variety of ways.

And fifth, the Christian big picture is a sweeping cosmic *drama* in which our individual life is swept up, and given a profound meaning and import, consequence and purpose.

Each of these five qualities of life is being affected in a variety of ways, some quite subtle, some rather obvious, by the technological age in which we live, and, in the chapters ahead, I will develop and explore the questions and challenges we must engage with if we are to emerge from it with the fullness of our humanity, dignity, and freedom intact. Only thus can we dedicate ourselves to the big picture of life and attain the kingdom and the joy for which we are made.

Chapter Four

The Monster Mashup

Human beings like monsters. Oddly enough, this is the first point I want to make about our central human reality and how it is being affected by technology.

It is just possible that this requires some explanation. But first, we do like monsters, right? I mean, we don't "like them" like them, as high schoolers are wont to say, but you know what I mean. Frankenstein and Dracula, the creature from the Black Lagoon and the Boogeyman — the whole bloodthirsty band of brothers warms the cockles of our hearts somehow. Dragons and sea serpents and griffons and manticores — who doesn't want one for a pet, really? (Be honest!) Goblins and ghosts and ghouls and great sundry gangs and gaggles of grotesqueries gladden us, give us god-honest glee.

Simply put, we like 'em.

Among the varied annals of monsters passed down to us through the tradition of fantastic literature, whether it be the great traditions of Greek and Roman myths or the more homely folk traditions of pre-Christian Europe, there is a certain category that has always held great fascination for us, a great motif that runs wide and deep from the oldest myths of Babylon and Greece down to Harry Potter.

Have you ever noticed how many of the monsters we know and love are hybrid creatures of one kind or another? In other words, how often we creative human beings make up a monster by combining two or more different species into one?

Centaurs and harpies, Pegasus and the Little Mermaid, fauns and werewolves — there is a long human tradition of delight or delightful horror in the creature who is both one thing and another, who combines two or more very different elements in a single life.

Now why would that be? I mean, I can understand our fascination for the creatures who look human but are not (vampires, giants, gorgons), who are us-but-not-us in other words (and who more often than not like to eat us . . . but that's another story), or the creatures who are like the animals we love, but all weirded out (Cerberus, phoenixes, the Nemean lion), but what's up with the Minotaur? The Sphinx?

I maintain that we love hybrids because when we look at them, we're really looking at ourselves in a funhouse mirror. That's why we are so taken with these creatures.

You see, we are those fantastic monsters, we human beings. Yes, it is us: we are those hybrids, those chimeras, those siren-satyr-centaur freaks. It is Us, Dear Reader — we, we are the Monsters, bwaahahhahhah!

Ahem. Excuse me — I've been reading too many nineteenth-century gothic novels lately.

But it is a fact. The whole human race is one big too-bizarre-to-believe Island-of-Dr.-Moreau experiment. Ah, but we have been cooked up, not in the laboratory of a mad scientist, but by the infinite wisdom of the Creative Intellect of our Father.

For it has been laid down from the beginning of the natural order, that among all the beings known to exist there are two strictly separate principles. There are two modes of being, two ways of existing that are completely different and operate by completely different sets of properties, rules, laws.

There is matter, and then there is spirit. Both (in the Judeo-Christian understanding) are good; both come from the creative will of God. But they are utterly different from one another.

Matter for its part is characterized by its seemingly infinite plasticity. It is pliable, able to be chopped up, schlepped around (I use the technical term here), combined and re-combined into all manners of shapes and sizes. Along with that pliability, it has a stubborn adherence to the laws of time and space; it is rooted, like a mountain, in its own placement at this moment, even if a nanosecond later it will be equally rooted someplace else.

Spirit, meanwhile, flies at the speed of thought to the ends of the earth, to the farthest reaches of the cosmos. And while speeding along blowing where it will (it's like the wind, to paraphrase the philosopher Patrick Swayze), it remains indivisible, impliable. Spiritual being perpetually expresses itself in the great thematic statement that echoes the Spirit of all spirits: "I am!" is the constant cry of each spiritual being.

And the human person is this bizarre and frightful hybrid, this mashup, this fantastic chimerical monster, the circus freak of the universe, this cosmic leap into the unthinkable. "And the Lord God formed man from the dust of the ground, and breathed into his nostrils the breath of life; and man became a living soul." (*Genesis* 2:7).

Body and soul, matter and spirit. That's us! The centaur, the mermaid, the winged horse, the creature combining in himself two principles of being, and somehow expressing a single life in this that forges the two principles into a complex and startlingly beautiful unity.

This unity however, has not always been appreciated. To say the least. From as early as we have written records of human efforts to understand our condition and identity, there has been a criticism, if you will, of the divine idea of man. We human beings have never been terribly sure that it was such a great idea to combine matter and spirit in this way, and have patiently explained this to God many times over. But (the poor old Guy!), He doesn't seem to get it, and keeps churning us out by the millions: seven billion strong at last count, just including the ones currently walking around.

Dualism is the name of this great philosophical-theological-mystical objection raised in the courts of human thought to the divine folly. God says (out of context, I realize), "What I have joined, let no man put asunder." We reply, "Well, now wait one cotton-pickin' minute here — we don't really like this idea. It's not comfortable! It's weird! All the other creatures are either one or the other, and they all look at us kind of funny, you know! And it's not such fun, being looked at funny by an angel or a Golden Retriever. Asunder away, sez me!"

And so we try to think of something better, something that will fix the problem. There are all the various strains of Gnosticism or Manichaeism, in which the flesh is created by an evil demiurge, and spirit alone is created by God. In some versions of this, original sin is not so much the disobedience of our first parents, but the actual creation of the physical universe, which then traps little bits of divine stuff into these stinky sweaty yucky slimy bodies. Salvation in these systems consists in liberation from the body, escaping the torments of physicality and re-absorption into the divine sphere. Buddhism, while it is much more philosophically elaborate and ethically nuanced than what we know of these ancient systems, shares this view of salvation and liberation.

Meanwhile, the flesh has always had its partisans, although for obvious reasons they are less likely to write long learned tomes about the rejection of spirit. They would have to sober up first, for one thing. The happy (?) hedonist is fundamentally one who also sees through bleary bloodshot eyes the dualism of flesh and spirit, and opts for the flesh side of the equation. The next round (hic!) is on me, lads!

And so it goes, down through the centuries. Dualism has been one of the "hardy perennials" of human thought and life. This bears witness to the fact that our body-soul unity is strange to us; we experience it as two very different things jammed together somehow. Often, people who know very little about the history of thought (and who, in fact, may be relative strangers to the practice of thought, too), casually assign blame to Christianity for the dualistic strain of human life, and especially for the longstanding theme of hostility towards the body.

They ignore the profound influence of Gnosticism in the pagan world that received the Gospel. Christianity may at times have been infected by this Gnostic virus, but Gnosticism is not its source, and in fact Christianity holds within itself the cure: "God saw everything He had made, and said that it is very good . . . and the Word became flesh, and dwelt among us" (*Genesis* 1:31, *John* 1:14).

Meanwhile, in the post-medieval, post-Christian world, dualism is resurgent. Descartes called the human person a "ghost in a machine." The real person is the soul, the immaterial being, and the body is simply a machine, an instrument. This Cartesian view of humanity remains influential. Modern deconstructionist gender theories explicitly adopt such an instrumentalist view of the human body: genital morphology is irrelevant to the sexual identity of the person, and you can fashion and refashion your body and define your own gender identity however you like based on some interior "real you."

To say the least, this is not the Christian vision. You are not some detached observer using your body for various purposes as a tool. Your body is you; your soul is you; you are body and soul together. This is why the resurrection of the body is such an essential Christian dogma. We are not fully present to the glory of God in heaven until we are bodily present to it, because we are not fully ourselves so long as our bodies and souls are separated.

The unity of soul and body, apart from its heavenly consummation in the Beatific Vision, where our "our own eyes shall see him" (Job 19:27), is also essential to our being fully alive and engaged and vibrant in our life on earth.

All human knowledge begins in the body. Everything we know begins in the senses, information entering our eyes and ears and noses and skin. The awesome power of the human soul and its unity to the body is its ability to draw immaterial truth out of material sensations — not only the truth of the physical objects that surround the person, but universal truths about God, about the soul itself, the nature of good and evil, etc.

Knowledge begins in the senses, in the body, and terminates in the mind's possession of immaterial truth. This spiritual grasp of truth in turn guides our choices that are expressed in our bodily actions, so that we shape our material world according to the demands of truth and goodness.

And so, God, in creating this fabulous monster "man," has created a creature that can both know and love the world He made, and join with Him in its ongoing creation, becoming co-creators with God in our material existence. And this crazy mixed-up mashed-up creature man, then, bears witness in his body-soul unity to the intrinsic unity and harmony of all God has made, matter and spirit both, and the unity of all God has made with its Maker.

As the constant theme of dualism bears witness to, however, this unity of mind and body is fragile, constantly imperiled by our fallen disordered condition. Our minds tend to wander, even if (being weak!) they may not get very far. By the wandering of the mind, I'm not thinking of creative imagination or speculative intelligence — these are proper actions of our mind that bear fruit in the creation of beauty or in deeper possession of truth.

But we all know about that abstraction of the mind where it goes places that bear no good fruit. Fantasy, vain speculation, idle curiosity — all of this is the mind's flight from incarnate reality. The body, meanwhile, has its own rejection of the mind. There is the indiscipline of the appetites, in which our bodies "want what they want," pursuing pleasure to the detriment of the full truth and goodness.

And there is simple physical laziness. Our

spirits are made to embrace universal reality. Our minds, by their very nature, expand outward to the apprehension of the true, the good, the beautiful in their fullness. Our bodies tend to resist this, seeking to stay rooted in the immediate, craving the easy. We are made to ascend the heights of Being, even unto the contemplation of God; sometimes, to be honest, I just want to settle for a burger and fries, and maybe a cold beer to go with it.

And so, we are always at risk of becoming fragmented — our minds here, our bodies there. And this is a diminishment of our humanity, ultimately. Our minds are meant to be expressed and operative through the actions of the body; our bodies are to be animated and elevated by the operation of the mind. Neither mind without body or body without mind bears fruit in the fullness of life we are made for, which is the communion of love with God and neighbor.

So we have a fundamental human problem, one that is always with us, but which is at the very least potentially being made worse by the all-pervasive presence of information technology. For all of its obvious benefits and potential for goodness, the internet is a way of being in the world that tends towards the fragmentation of body and soul, a way of life that tends to be highly disembodied.

The internet tends to reduce our relationship to information to the bare physical minimum: words and images enter our mind through our eyes. The backlit flat screen is a washed out, minimalistic encounter with the world, abstract and abstracting us from the "full body contact" of man in the world.

We are in contact with the world, for sure, as we interact with the flat screen. But it is a world — cyber-space — forged entirely by other minds. Mind meets mind in the little flat screen of the device. Yes, we use keyboards and mouse pads and other physical impedimenta to enter this mind-to-mind engagement (although the pioneers advancing technology to the next level are promising great things: nanochips implanted in our brains so that we directly control our computers by thought alone, and other such fantastical scenarios). Meanwhile, the necessary physical tools of the technological day have been standardized so that they impinge only minimally on the strictly mental exercise of the digital encounter.

When we look at modern social networking and communication, we see another aspect of this same disembodied quality. "Come and hang out with your friends on e-mail or Facebook, chat rooms, or by constant text messaging." It sounds great, and all very sociable and chummy, and it is, sort of.

But all of these are inherently artificial environments where we meet one another primarily with text. Words appear on a flat screen, but do they really communicate the real person behind the words? When someone types LOL in a message, are they really laughing out loud? They may actually be clinically depressed, or angry. Who can tell? The washed-out, abstract, disembodied nature of modern social networking and communication is woefully deficient in terms of a true person-to-person encounter.

And there is a passivity that enters in with this kind of disembodied life. To take in information through the senses is unavoidable, and indeed a very good thing; the contemplative stance to reality is necessary, if we are to live in truth. But this taking in of reality is meant to translate to active engagement with the world. And there is something about sitting in front of that flat screen that does not easily translate to that kind of activity.

We click on a link, read or watch whatever is there, and then click on the next link. Then scroll around Facebook and leave comments here and there, then click on another link. Words and images flow across the surface of our minds through our eyes . . . and then what? Does it really enter in? Do we gain true understanding of our world, which then empowers us to stand up from our computers and plunge into positive action? I'm not talking about social activism necessarily or overt charitable works. I'm talking about something as mundane (although it is nothing of the sort, really) as cooking supper for your family with renewed love and energy because you have been renewed in your vision of the true, the good, the beautiful by the action of your mind.

Does that happen very often, living in front of a flat screen? I don't know. Maybe it does! But this is the kind of question we have to ask ourselves, I would suggest. Does this technology tend to abstract our minds from our bodies, and if so, does it do this in a way that yields creativity and deepening of understanding, or does it simply fragment us?

Now, there are good objections to the concerns I raise. For example, what about books? Books are a flat screen of sorts, after all — words on a page, merely. What about TV? Another flat screen, and haven't we all been raised on it? And it hasn't done us any harm . . . oh, wait a minute, uhh . . . OK, forget that objection.

But the point remains that there are lots of ways our minds go where our bodies don't, and so what's the problem with information technology? Why is it uniquely fragmenting?

Well, first of all, who among us who had a vigilant mother never once heard in childhood, "Why do you have your nose in a book?" or "Are you going to sit there watching TV all day? — go out and play, for crying out loud." And actions to match the words, as we got tossed on our juvenile behinds into the back yard to *do something.*

In other words, it has always been the case that **we need a balance between the passive taking in of information through the eyes and ears, and the positive engagement with the world**. It has never been a good thing (I admit reluctantly, inveterate reader that I am) to live with one's nose in a book; it has certainly never been remotely a good thing to veg out in front of a TV for hours on end.

The trouble with the digital age is that more and more of life is being co-opted by the flat screen and its protocols. Your friends actually are hanging out on Facebook, and so rather than meeting for coffee or some other real activity, you have to go and stare at that damn screen again. Information that you might in the past have had to roam around looking for is all available now on the tiny screen of your smart phone, and so there you are, sitting at home, staring at it. Games, which may in the past have actually involved being in the same room as other people and, you know, socializing as you rolled dice or shuffled cards or did charades, are now (yes, wait for it!) on that flat screen once again.

Playing beach volleyball on a Wii may seem as good as the real thing, but is it? When your feet actually touch the gritty sand and you can smell the surf and hear the whoosh of the ball as it soars towards you and you leap up to spike it and miss and it hits you in the face, and you're lying there on the gritty sand and blood runs down your face from your broken nose, and some cute girl in a bathing suit administers first aid and . . . well, it's a bit more than a flat screen, really, isn't it? A bit more "whee!" and an experience of "we" than one can get from a Wii. Being there — that's my point. Doing it, and not a simulation of it.

The disembodied quality of the flat screen and all its manifestations is not a bad thing; it is not wrong and it may not be harmful, as long as we know its limits. And that's the precise word: it is *limited*. We have to be aware of that.

And so it has to be kept in check. If your whole life, or an undue portion of it anyhow, is spent with your mind on the flat screen and your body somewhere else, then the tendency of mind and body to fragment is going to be accentuated. It's a question we each have to ask ourselves, and probably everyone has to establish a balance for himself. But we have to know the risk of fragmentation and the impoverishment of our lives if we do not counter it.

So, basically, turn off the computer once in a while, or the i-pad, or the smart phone! Be where your body is! Bake some bread! Chase a soccer ball around a field! Play a board game! Have a conversation with someone who is actually in the same room as you. Laugh out loud, don't LOL around all the time. Get down on your knees and pray (just like yesterday!). Write a book (hey, what a great idea!). Make a baby (if you're married, LOL).

It really is a question of **spending the bulk of our time with body and mind in the same place**. It is a question of experiencing life directly, of our whole person — body, mind, soul, spirit — living in the one reality at one time. It's a question of the integration of our humanity, of our personal identity, as a solid whole, one person immersed in the world, taking it in to know it and love it, and pouring out the fruits of this love and knowledge in a fully alive, engaged human life.

Chapter Five

Virtual Reality

OK — so are all your bodies and minds together? Double check now! Pinch yourself! OK. So, we're all here? Present and accounted for? Good. Because that brings us directly to the second aspect of our humanity I want to discuss.

That is the quality of **living in the *here-and-now***. Attentiveness, presence, living in the moment — this too is essential to the human reality.

We are by nature and necessity temporal, spatial creatures — we are here, we are now. It's an obvious point, but important to appreciate. Because like our body-soul unity, it's not quite a given, not entirely.

Our spiritual nature, our intellect, allows us to roam mentally all of time and space, to look up at the stars and down into subatomic particles, to ponder the cave paintings of Lascaux and what they reveal of the ancient past or indulge in speculative imagination about the far-off future.

All of this has a proper place in our life, but, all the same, there remains the fundamental reality. That is: I am here, typing furiously on my laptop. You are here, reading this book and probably hoping I get to something resembling a point before much longer. Hello you! What's the weather like in the future?

Our spiritual natures carry us all over the place, but our bodies remain here and now. This **presence to the here and now is vitally important to our human flourishing**. Isn't it true that we have an amazing ability to *not* pay attention to where we are, to absent ourselves from it, to dissociate, to shut down?

Of course, there are all sorts of reasons for that, good and bad. Sometimes the present moment is simply too painful or confronting for us. Denial and dissociation are survival tactics in the midst of overwhelming traumatic events. Only a sadist would extol the virtues of living in the moment, of being alive to the here and now to someone in the middle of being tortured or sexually assaulted. Tragically, though, victims of trauma and abuse can become trapped in a pattern of dissociation and denial that carries over into the rest of their lives, wreaking a wide swath of havoc in their relationships and interior wellbeing.

We also know that many people live in the past, in regret or guilt, grieving for a lost happiness or lacerating themselves for real or imagined failures and sins. Others live in the future, burdened by the anxiety of trying to plan against every eventuality or paralyzed into inactivity by the fear of making a mistake, or dreaming of how things might be next year, if only. . . .

Still others live in unreality, in fantasy and illusion. Boredom, a lack of meaning, spiritual emptiness, or intolerable loneliness and deep unhappiness drive people out of the real and into the imagined, whether their own inner fantasy life or the banal entertainments of television and movies.

A person who lives fully present to the present moment at all times is rare. One who I was fortunate enough to know was a member of Madonna House named Jim Guinan, now dead several years. Jim was an elderly man when I knew him, an Irish American from Michigan, full of that unique blend of wild humor and heartfelt piety once common among the Irish, now become sadly rare. After many years of service to the inner-city poor and some years spent as one of the directors of the MH apostolate, he spent the last fifteen years of his life as a poustinik[8], a sort of modified hermit within a communal setting.

Jim as I knew him had an extraordinary capacity to love each person who crossed his path. Simply put, **he was utterly present to whoever was in front of him**. When you met Jim, you would swear that you had made his day; running into you was just the greatest thing that had happened to him; you were the most important person in the world. But if you noticed, you would see that the next person he ran into would get exactly the same treatment. And it was not even slightly put on or fake (in a close-knit Christian community like Madonna House, that doesn't fly for a minute!).

He would joke a bit with those who liked jokes, give a word of encouragement to the ones who looked sad or tired ("It's a great life, old boy," he would say, "if you just keep plugging and doing the best you can!"),

---

[8] The word "poustinik" is derived from the Russian word "poustinia," desert, and evokes the early desert fathers of the Church, "poustinia" being a potent symbol of prayer, silence, and solitude at the heart of Christian prayer and spirituality.

tease those who looked far too serious for their own good, perform little acts of service and gracious courtesy, especially for the women (he was a great opener of doors and helper-on of coats) — always with that Irish twinkle in his eyes.

Going through each day, utterly present and warm and welcoming to each person he met, the ones he had known for decades and the new guest just arrived off the bus. Meeting each with a total attentiveness to whom they were and where they were at and what they might need that he could give. Day after day living like this, for years, and in between encounters with "the most important person in the world," working quietly away at various humble tasks, and praying his rosary incessantly. I only knew Jim in his elder years; those who knew him when he was younger say he was always like that. It was a remarkable experience to live with him, and he remains for me my personal benchmark of Christian love and holiness.

It is this presence to the present moment that is so important for us, for our humanity, for living a genuine human life in the world. Why is that? We have to go back to the "big picture" to understand how really important it is. We can all appreciate, especially if we have known someone like Jim Guinan, that this mode of radical presence to the here and now is beautiful and life giving. But to fully grasp the vital necessity of it, we have to remember what it's all about — that big picture.

The whole point of life, remember, is to live in a totality of communion with God. Flowing from our communion with God, we can live in communion with one another. Now, God is eternal — outside of time. He is also infinite — unbound by limits of place. There is no "where and when" in God; strictly speaking, no here and now with the All-Eternal and All-Present One.

But He is also the All-Real One, Reality itself, Being itself. Being Real, the only "time and place" in which we can find Him and so enter into communion with Him is in real time and real place. And the only reality we have is our current temporal-spatial one. So **God the Real One is present to us only in our reality, which is where we are, here and now**.

Our communion with one another is equally a here and now event. Think about it — the only love you can offer anyone in your life is your choice to be loving now. "Now" is the only place you are, and you have no freedom of choice, no capacity for self-determination except here and now. Love now, because now is all you've got.

This is the reason why the making of a vow is an inherently religious act. I do not possess the future; how can I promise or vow to love this person for the rest of my life? How can I vow to live a consecrated life, whether the consecration of marriage or of some form of religious life or priestly ministry? It is only by placing my will now to do this into the hands of God Who transcends time and holds my entire life in His one act of love and creative assent that my vowing to do anything is even meaningful, let alone true, good, and beautiful. Strictly speaking, I cannot choose to love God or another human being tomorrow, only now.

So the big picture of life really does come down to my choice, this minute, to pay attention to this person, to listen to that person, to work attentively at this task. The big picture is not a matter of some cosmic sweep of life that fills our minds and hearts to the exclusion of all trivial concerns; it is a question of whether I will smile and greet you, now, whether you will lend a helping hand to a frazzled co-worker, now, or be kind to a stranger, now. Even all our ordinary daily promises, which are made without vows, are choices, here and now, to be loving by assuring the ones to whom we make them that we care enough about them to be concerned about their future needs, as well as about their immediate ones. Here and now — that's where the big picture is found, or it is found nowhere and never.

And so in regard to technology, this vital presence to the here and now, to the real, raises the question of "virtual reality". What does that phrase mean, exactly? Virtual means almost, but not quite. So, the almost real? An experience of reality that is not quite it, but comes close?

It's a problematic term, one lacking a clear referent, in my opinion. Clearly it means something definite to computer programmers and researchers pushing back the frontiers of the computational experience: the increasingly sophisticated efforts to create a sort of "Tron-like" fully nuanced world of sight, sound, feel, and color, where the user's entire field of perception is absorbed by the machine-generated stimuli, creating an alternative world of sensation, including the self-sensation of one's own physical extension and morphology.

Now that's all very interesting, and I applaud the extraordinary genius that goes into this technological achievement. And it may well have some very useful purpose in real-world terms, unclear as this may be to me right now. But in light of the vital importance of the here and now to human flourishing, I want to develop this notion of virtual reality in a slightly different fashion.

It is possible, I maintain, to be surfing merrily away on the internet, to be plugged into a half dozen gadgets and gizmos and media devices, senses stimulated in all directions at once, and yet not be in virtual reality. At the same time, both you and I could be in virtual reality right now, this very moment, as I write this book and as you read it. Virtual reality as I want to discuss it in this book is this whole business of "reality, but not quite." Being almost in the real world, but not entirely.

Virtual reality is about our choice to be present to God and to neighbour, or to go far, far away into a world of our own making. It's really a question of love. At every moment of our lives, there is a demand of charity. At every moment of our lives, there is an action of the Spirit of God, calling us to some response. At every moment of our lives, there is a present that we are to be present to, so as to respond appropriately in love and justice. So the question of how virtual our present reality is hinges upon how present we are to the depths of what is happening within and around us right now. In short, are you loving right now? If not, you are not really present to reality; you are in virtual reality.

So, if we can truly say that we are present to God and to neighbor, to the demands of justice and charity and the action of the Spirit as we buzz about in our gadget-filled environment, then technology holds no problem for us in this regard. But I think it is worth asking ourselves honest, searching questions about that. All these gadgets are very noisy, very busy, very clamorous for our attention, and are really good at pulling us here, there, and all about the town.

The constant flow of information from around the world is all very interesting and may lead me to prayer and heightened awareness of what's going on everywhere . . . or it may not. It may just distract me from the real people I live with who, in fact, need me to love them and lay down my life for them right now.

Computer games present themselves here as a real question. So what's wrong with playing a game? Nothing, inherently. Nor is there anything wrong with playing a game in which you are the only player. "Thou shalt not play solitaire" is not written anywhere in our holy books.

A bit more problematic, though, are these hyper-simulated and super-stimulating video games that immerse you in another imaginary world of action and sights and sounds and colors and adventures. And, all of a sudden, five hours have gone by, out of my life, never to return. Where have I been? What have I done with these hours? What has this game done to me? Is Halo helping me to obtain a real halo? Where are all these games taking me? Anywhere good? Am I here? Am I present? Can I be?

This is something we need to think about. Games are good in themselves. The good of a game is the good of relaxation, recreation. But this good of relaxation has to occupy its proper place in life. All lesser goods have to be subordinated and ordered towards higher goods. We are to relax and recreate so as to recover our energies, to be able to love and serve, to be able to be attentive and generous. Does playing a computer game for hours on end order us towards that goal?

We all know people — young guys in particular — who at least appear to get really addicted to video games, spending hours and hours in a fantasy world, more often than not a hyper-violent one. (Of course that is a separate issue altogether — what is the content of these video games? Some of them are quite vile, but that's another story.) But I think that many of us, seeing this kind of addictive compulsive use of video games have been rather disquieted at the picture of our sons or brothers or nephews or cousins so deeply immersed in these worlds.

Perhaps we have not always had the vocabulary to say what's wrong with it. I hope this chapter has shed some light on the matter, and can open a dialogue about the proper place and limits of gaming in general and computer gaming in particular (assuming you can wrestle them away from the X-box long enough for a coherent conversation to occur).

But the question all of us have to answer is this: where am I? Where is the technology I use taking me? Am I here? Am I now? Am I present to you? To God? It takes a lot, you know, to really be present in that way, the way that makes us fully alive and loving in the here and now, that level of Guinan-esque presence and charity.

It takes a lot of interior quiet, a lot of inward attentiveness. It takes a lot of death to self and deep prayer. It takes a lot of vision, of faith that God is in fact waiting to meet us here and now in whatever it may hold for us. Do we have what it takes?

Is my heart quiet, my mind attentive to the demands of love and service in my little corner of the world? Am I ready and able to have that level of availability, that generosity of charity, that vision of faith?

If my use of technology detracts from any of that, I have to think about it! And, perhaps, I might just need to make different choices. Put down the joystick and seek a deeper joy. Drop the blogs and pick up the beads. Stop surfing and scrolling in favour of praying and fasting.

In other words, if the hyper-stimulated, taking-us-everywhere-all-at-once world of technology is detracting from my ability to be and love where I am, then, to put it very simply, maybe I need to do something else with my time and energy.

Chapter Six

Disunion Station

Union Station, Washington DC, 8:00 a.m. I am standing on the subway platform, surrounded by the mass of humanity. Government/business types in their power suits jostle up against gang-banging teenagers, conscientiously grungy hipsters intermingle with fresh-faced college kids. Not too many tourists at this hour — more the typical urban DC scene, that curious mixture of sleek well-groomed, well-dressed well-fed power interwoven with the extremes of gritty urban poverty. And me: a half-awake rather rumply Catholic priest, hair sticking up as usual and dressed in shabby well-worn black clerics, off for another day of graduate school wrassling with Aquinas, Bonaventure, and Duns Scotus, under the tutelage of the St. Joseph's Province Dominican friars who are all much, much smarter than me. On the platform and in the crowded train (yay, I got a seat today!), I'm getting the usual assemblage of startled looks, dirty looks, prolonged stares, sidelong glances, and the occasional smile of recognition that most priests are used to receiving in public. Or maybe they're just staring at my hair. I don't know.

Amongst this random assortment of humanity, though, there is one thing that unites almost everyone on the train. Eyes quickly fix on cell phone screens (the Dawn of the Tablets came just after my time in DC). Ears sprout buds or Bluetooth connections. The beat of rap music occasionally penetrates, barely audible, from some of these. Conversations abound, but hardly anyone is talking to anyone else who is actually on the train. Thumbs fly in a flurry of texting. Rich or poor, young or old, black or white, shabby or sleek, college bound or not; all wrap themselves in their digital cocoon and settle in for the morning commute.

If I had to say where this book on technology had its inception, where I started to think and pray about the machines we use and the effect they have on us, I would have to say it was my two years living in Washington DC, getting a Licentiate in Sacred Theology, riding the subway, walking around K Street, Pennsylvania Avenue, Georgetown, and the National Mall, immersed in that most technologically wired-in of American cities (although I understand there are cities in Asia that make DC look like a poor third-rate backwater in this matter).

I had much to ponder there because, of course, as a member of a community, Madonna House, with a promise of poverty, I didn't have any of those gadgets. I had a laptop for my studies, but that was it. So as I walked about and metroed my way around for two years, I had much occasion to behold and ponder another aspect of our humanity and its alteration by technology.

In fact, it is this next aspect of staying human that I am most concerned about in all the technological revolution. Since my years in Washington, and in the process of researching this book, I've read lots of the literature exploring the issues around technology. I've read books and articles sounding warnings about the disembodying effect or distracting tendencies of technology; I've read books about how the information age is making us dumber, more socially inept, and otherwise reducing our humanity to its extension in internet protocols and paradigms.

But I haven't yet seen my deepest

concern about technology addressed. Perhaps it's a bit insidious. I don't know why no one else but me seems to have written about this, but here is what I am personally most worried about in the technological age we live in.

Human beings are called to a certain *universality* of experience. In other words, we are called to be open to the world. We are made in God's image, made to have an attitude towards creation that is at least similar to His. And His attitude is that He loves everything He has made, and particularly every person He has made. We are called, then, to love everything and everyone. And the bare minimum of this love is expressed in a certain kind of *openness* to every other person.

We are also meant to be open to the whole experience of the world around us, both the world God created and the world our fellow human beings have fashioned. Catherine Doherty, the woman who founded Madonna House, placed great emphasis on our apostolic spirit of hospitality, on the open door, the welcoming presence. She talked about the need to have, not just hospitality of the home, but of the heart. This is more than just welcoming a guest into your home or sharing a meal with someone. It is a deep call to be present and open to what is *not you*, to what is different from you.

We are called to be present to the person sitting across from us, whoever they are: to what they say, what they think about things. We are to be present to the sights, sounds, and smells that come to us, whether they delight or appall us. This sounds like just another way of saying that we are to be present to the here and now. The different accent here, though, is that we are not in control of what is coming at us. Instead, we are just "taking it in" as it comes.

This is profoundly important to a proper human experience of reality. This kind of openness and presence to the other as other and to the out-of-our-control quality of the world as it comes to us moment by moment, plays an essential role in convincing us of one simple and essential truth about our lives.

Namely, that we are not God. We are not the masters of our own being and fate and truth. There is a whole world outside of us that we did not make, do not control; and (frankly, my dear) it doesn't seem to give a damn about our thoughts on the matter. Why is this so important? Well, what is it exactly that follows upon this encounter with the world?

Humility, that's what. And when we receive a little bit of humility, of the knowledge that we are just one little person in a very big world that goes on around us without consulting us, we begin to open up to God. Because maybe there's a Very Big Person who knows a little more about this world than we do. And from this openness to God comes everything else we long for: love, peace, and joy. Because that's what He brings those who stay open to Him.

So this is where I have a major concern about techno-culture. It is perfectly possible today for you to walk around all day, or at least when you're not on the job, wearing ear buds hooked to *your* i-pod playing precisely the songs *you* like and choose. You can walk around all day talking or texting on *your* cell phone to *your* little circle of friends, the small group of people who matter to *you*.

Then you can go home and crank up the internet and hang out in a chat room or Facebook or on this or that blog or whatever, where everyone thinks exactly like *you* about politics or religion or has the same hobbies and interests as *you*. Or, even if they don't, at any rate they are precisely the people you choose to "be with" on-line. And hey, if anyone says (or rather types) something you don't like, one click of the mouse ends the encounter. Buh bye, baby, I'm out of here! Click.

To an extent absolutely unprecedented in the history of the world, it is possible for almost anyone in the technological world to create a little bubble to inhabit where they are absolutely immersed in only those parts of the world that suit them, that they have chosen.

Of course, when we go to work it stands to reason that there we have to engage with the world as it is, not as we would like it to be. But this is seen increasingly as a necessary evil, not as something good in itself. And more and more we hear anecdotal evidence from employers and supervisors that at least some of the young people coming into the work force now in fact do expect the workplace to conform itself to their expectations and desires and are highly resistant and resentful when they find out it doesn't work that way.

In times past, only the very rich could expect the world to arrange itself to their likes and dislikes. And, frankly, it wasn't good for them! "It is easier for a camel to go through the eye of the needle than for a rich man to enter the kingdom of heaven" (*Matthew* 19:24). To be in total control of your world is spiritually perilous.

But this is the spiritually perilous world we increasingly inhabit today, and particularly that we allow our young ones to inhabit. Today you only have to talk to, or even notice the existence of, your friends and family, only listen to your music, only think your own thoughts. Google tailors its search results to your existing opinions and worldview, based on the links you've clicked on previously. Amazon showcases for you the books it thinks you might be interested in, based on prior purchases. Who you are and what you think about things slowly gets funnelled into an increasingly narrow track.

Pauline Kael, film reviewer for the *New York Times*, famously remarked in 1972 of her shock at Nixon's re-election: "But I don't know anyone who voted for him!"

More and more we can enter that kind of Kaelian insularity, that kind of world where everything we see, hear, and take in reflects back to us our own idea of reality. An endless hall of mirrors, a triumph of solipsism: technology doesn't have to take you into that kind of bubble, but it sure is good at it.

Ironically, it is in cities that we see this most clearly. It is ironic because the city is supposed to be the place of cosmopolitan expanse, the place where humanity in all its variety is thrown together into a rich varied tapestry of culture and taste. But, as the subway platform at Union Station shows us, this doesn't really happen that much. Everyone is immersed in his little world, no eye contact, no awareness of the other. This is not a new situation (people used to hide behind their newspapers!) but technology has ramped it up to a new level. From Union Station we have degraded to a profound state of disunion.

I think this has gone unremarked for the most part because to most people it seems like a perfectly normal state of affairs, an unavoidable by-product of city life. Who can be present to the teeming masses on subway and street? And who wants to be present to the ugly sights and sounds and smells of the modern urban landscape? Why not stick in the ear buds and listen to Mozart or Ella Fitzgerald, for crying out loud?

I think this situation is anything but normal, however, even if it does reflect a certain tendency humanity has always shown in the urban landscape. In fact, I think the situation we are facing is extremely dangerous, threatening our long-term ability to live in a peaceful civil society. I will get to that in a moment, but, on the way there, I want to address this whole business of ugliness that many would invoke to justify tuning out the world. Who wants to look at all these ugly people and hear all these ugly sounds, etc., etc.?

The medieval scholastic notion of the transcendentals is key here, believe it or not. To the medievals, everything that existed, everything that possessed being was good (insofar as it enjoyed the fullness of the sort of being it was), and true (an attribute I described in Chapter Two — true as in presenting itself to our minds). Some of the medievals added that goodness and truth taken together yield a third transcendental, a third quality common to all existing things.

Namely, beauty. Everything is beautiful in that the goodness inherent in that being shines forth in its true self-disclosure to the beholder.

In other words, everything is beautiful, in its own way. Yes, at least some of the medievals were, in fact, hippies. They would add (proving it by strict logical analysis!) that all you need is love, and they would also agree unhesitatingly, that there is in fact actually nothing wrong with peace, love, and understanding.

Well, as I was wrassling with Bonaventure, etc., over all these matters in Washington, surrounded by all those smart Dominicans, I decided it was time for a practicum on this. If everything, and everyone, is in fact beautiful, then I should be able with a little hard work to see this in everyone. Beauty that is not perceptible is not beauty. So I began to covertly (I hope ...) look at the people surrounding me on the subway, playing a game I called "spot the beauty." They probably didn't notice me doing this since they were all staring at their cell phones.

And I found out — gosh darnit! — that the medievals were right, actually. Everyone I looked at did have some beauty, somewhere in his being. There was that fat middle-aged businessman over there, no example at all of masculine beauty, but then, you know, he would smile, and he had a really nice smile. Transformed his face: really beautiful! The old lady, one big wrinkle at first glance, but then I would notice her hands, age-worn, translucent, lovely in shape and in character. Then there was that rather homely and shapeless young girl over there . . . but look at her eyes: her eyes are beautiful. One day, a man who was horribly disfigured got on the train. He appeared to be a burn victim, and was a terrible sight, really. But again, look at his eyes — and the suffering, the patient endurance, the dignity in them. I still remember that; one of the most beautiful things I have ever seen, I think.

As I reflected on my "spot the beauty" game, I realized I had needed to do something first in order to find out that the medieval philosophers were quite correct, that everything and everyone actually is beautiful. I had needed to separate the concept of "beauty" from the concept of sexual attractiveness. In other words, beauty could not be equated with a desire for possession of the person on my part. And this, I think, was an important discovery.

When we say, "Oh this is ugly or she is ugly or he is so very, very ugly," I maintain that we are evaluating him/her/it by the narrow criterion of whether or not we *want* him/her/it. There is a not-so-subtle egoism at play here. I don't want you, so you are ugly. Get out of my sight, you! Oh, really?

You know, it may just be that I am not the grand adjudicator of desirability for the universe and all that fills it. Maybe there is another One Who is such a judge, and Who clearly desires every single thing He has seen fit to create. Maybe everything *is* beautiful, in His own way of seeing it. So this argument that urbanites and others tend to make that we need to wrap ourselves in the digital cocoon because we are constantly surrounded by such hideous, hideous reality speaks less to the actual truth of things and more to our own need to break out of the solipsism of our narrow judgments.

There is no ugliness, not in the things themselves, not if we look at them correctly. Ugliness comes in only when there is no love, when there is hatred or cold indifference, or when the truth and goodness of a creature is obscured in one way or another beyond our capacity to perceive it. But even there, we who are Christians at least should know that the human response to that "ugly" reality is not to withdraw ourselves, but to be present in that place as the very presence of God's love and compassion there.

This withdrawal, this wrapping into a digital cocoon made up of what we like, what we desire, what we deem beautiful because it directly pleases us, amplified and accelerated by the technology that makes this so easy, so all-encompassing, is, I believe, placing us in a deep and immediate peril.

The human race is at risk of lapsing into a sort of neo-tribalism that I fear endangers our ability to form a coherent and functioning civil society, that places our very ability to live together in peace at risk. We are dividing up into little tribal groups who have as little to do with each other as is physically possible. Technology — ear buds, Bluetooths, tablets and all that jazz — makes it possible to have very little indeed to do with each other.

This is very dangerous. In the tribal so-

cieties of the ancient world, it was understood that a person only had moral
obligations or indeed any connection at all
to those in his or her own tribe. Frequently,
the tribe's own name for itself simply translated into "the people." All those outside the
tribe were "the others," not really people at
all. As such, they were outside the circle of
moral concern. Your neighbour was someone of your own people. Often, those not of
the tribe could be killed or raped or de-
spoiled of their goods with impunity.

It has been a long journey, never perfectly accomplished except in the great saints of
our race, for human beings to break out of
this. The notion that we only have obligations towards the members of our little
circle, our tribe or family or village goes
deep in us. The idea of the brotherhood of
man, of the human family, is a fragile one.

It is difficult for a human being to really
hold on to this idea that I am deeply con-
nected to every human being on the face of
the earth. Everyone is my brother, my sister.

Technology, which at first glance seems
to hold out the promise of total global con-
nectivity, of a shared global culture,
ironically threatens to reduce us back to

utter stone-age tribalism. In a world where I can block out anything and anyone who doesn't conform to my ideas and likes, I can easily lapse into a moral universe in which nobody else even exists except my own people. Certainly, nobody but my own people has any claim on me, any moral obligation to demand of me.

The technological world, by enabling us to avoid almost entirely any part of reality that does not please us, opens the door to a fragmented, polarized world where only my little group matters to me.

For a Christian, this cannot stand. In Christ, everyone is "my people." **In Christ, there is not one atom of creation that is alien to me, that is not to be loved, embraced, received.** In Christ, the very rattle of the subway car, the sounds of traffic, the smell of the subway and the street are the world I am to go forward to in love and prayer. In Christ, the wrinkled old lady or smelly street person or eyebrow-pierced teenager or sleek professional sitting across from me is my sister, my brother.

Technology, if it is to serve our humanity, cannot be used to create a bubble world where we control everything coming into our senses. This is not a human way to live, not if we understand the big picture of humanity.

We are not meant to live in a pod, "i-" or otherwise! Shuck it off, and open up to the world God has put you in, the whole world, the good, the bad, and the (to you) ugly. Why should you? Because that's where God is, waiting for you among His creatures whom He loves. And it's only by moving through the world with God that we stay human in the midst of it all.

Chapter Seven

Human Enough

What's your relationship status? Married? Engaged? In a relationship? Single? Facebook wants to know! You have to choose one. Ah, gee . . . help me out here — I really don't know what to choose!

Someone suggested to me, humorously, that the only appropriate choice on the relationship status menu Facebook gives me, belonging as I do to the tightly knit community of Madonna House, with over 200 members both male and female, clerical and lay, would be "It's complicated!"

I don't feel single, somehow, even though no, I am not married nor as a celibate Roman Catholic priest am I currently or ever going to be "seeing" anyone. I share my bathroom with way too many people to qualify as a "bachelor" in the ordinary understanding of the term. It can get complicated, especially five minutes before we pile into the car to head over to the main house for morning prayer.

Yes indeed, it is complicated, this whole relationship business, and not just in a community like Madonna House, or in the fragmented post-modern world, either. To be in relationship, to be *with* another person, in any fashion, is a complex dance indeed. Every person you have ever met in your life is a universe unto himself: thoughts, memories, ideas, experiences, emotions, physicality, and the mysterious spiritual undercurrent that pervades it all — the enigmatic "I" that each person is and bears through all the outward manifestations of personality.

It is complicated, and difficult. I live in community with 200 "universes," 200 ways of looking at the same reality, 200 people coming from different worlds and responding in wildly different ways to the common world of Madonna House in which we have all chosen to live together. United in essentials by our Catholic faith and a certain Gospel vision of life given to us by our founder Catherine de Hueck Doherty, we honestly, really have little else in common with one another.

We sometimes joke, in a serious kind of way, that God has asked us to try to live together in peace and love to show the rest of the world that if this motley assemblage of random oddballs can do it, so can everyone else (no offence, MH members reading this book! Love ya! Love ya all!).

Ahem. Anyhow. All of this is to establish myself, if I may, as something of an expert in the field of human relationships. Celibates are often dismissed as knowing nothing whatsoever about these matters (since of course to abstain from sexual intercourse necessarily means that one has no human contact with anyone, anytime, anywhere, right?). I don't know how it works in other communities, but in MH, we are IN RELATIONSHIP pretty much all the time, and yes, IT IS COMPLICATED!!! Sorry for shouting.

Wouldn't it be great if we could just make it a bit easier? It would be so splendid if we each walked around with some kind of little hand-held tool: call it, oh I don't know, a rat or vole or shrew or some other kind of small rodent-like creature. And it could have a button on it that we could, say, point and click at, well, a little "x" or something conveniently located at the top right corner of one another's heads. You know, just so we could get out of difficult encounters quickly. Joni Mitchell had a song back in the day, "You Turn Me On (Like a Radio)." Wouldn't it be great if we could turn "complicated" people off like a TV? Click: goodbye!

It would be so much easier if, instead of

being confronted with the person, with all their verbal and non-verbal cues, all their emotional energy and complex thought patterns expressing in manifold subtle ways we could just . . . oh, I don't know, write short messages at each other, maybe on some kind of portable electronic device. IMHO, it would be simpler. OMG, would it evcr! Maybe you disagree (YMMV), but I think it would be gr8. The thought of conducting all my relationships that way makes me LOL with delight. TTYL! ♥ ya! Woot woot. See — much easier, if rather more annoying. But hey, if I'm annoying you, you can always turn me off like a TV — it's the little "x" at the top right corner of my. . . . And so it goes. We all know that the relationship thing is hard. Not just because people are complicated (although that really is it, in a nutshell) but because these complicated people can . . . well, they can hurt us pretty bad, right? They can reject us. Misunderstand us. Betray us, intentionally or unintentionally. Lie to us. Say wounding things to us. Let us down when we need them most.

Even in a truly Christian community, which Madonna House is, where people are trying earnestly to love one another and be kind and charitable, hurt happens. And there is always, in human life, a tendency in the face of that to withdraw, to pack yourself, your *real* self, deep down away somewhere in a safe place, and present a mere surface to others, a glossy sheen, a good front, a friendly but somewhat mechanical exterior. One that cannot be hurt so much, because it's not really you. One cobbled together from the latest cool Internet catch-phrases or memes, one always smiling, always having a gr8 time. Not so much Facebook as Mask-my-Facebook. My-empty-space. i-Amnotreallyhere. Because as the saying goes, you cannot spell Twitter without the word "it" — and these forms of social networking often subtly substitute "thou" with "it" in myriad ways.

LOL — not.

Sherry Turkle writes in her wonderful book *Alone Together: Why We Expect More from Technology and Less from One Another*[9] about the growing prevalence of robotic devices pro-grammed to simulate pets, babies, companions for the elderly, and even basic caregivers in hospitals or nursing homes. She writes of how people using these devices, even though they

---

[9] Sherry Turkle, *Alone Together: Why We Expect More from Technology and Less from One Another,* (New York: Basic Books, 2011).

know full well that they are machines simply acting as their algorithmic software has designed them to do, nonetheless relate to them as if they were sentient beings, genuine creatures with whom they can be in a relationship.

A psychologist who for decades has studied the impact of emerging technology on human beings, Turkle describes how children who played with toys such as Tamagotchis or Furbies "[used] the phrase 'alive enough' as a measure not of biological readiness but of relational readiness."[10] Elsewhere, in discussing the misgivings raised by robot nurses or caregivers, she relates arguments some make that human caregivers often only "pretend to care,"[11] about their patients. That being the case, what's the difference between a robot nurse and a human one?

Alive enough, relational readiness, pretending to care — what is at stake here is the most fundamental reality of our humanity. "It is not good for man [the human person] to be alone," (*Genesis* 2:18). This is the first thing in creation, says God, that is "not good." Really, the only person who could ever have accurately used the current expression "It's all good" is

---

[10] Ibid., 28-9.
[11] Ibid., 124.

God, and even then, only in the period lasting from *Genesis* 1:1 to 2:17. After that, something not good is introduced into the world, and that not-good-thing is isolation. It is profoundly significant in the *Genesis* account that it is only with the introduction of humanity, and hence freedom, that created beings can be good or not good, can choose to be what they should be or fail to become this. But then, what should we be?

Together, that's what. **We are made for relationship, for communion, and there are no exceptions to this.** Even religious hermits must have some human relationships, and know themselves to be called into the solitude of God precisely with and for the sake of the whole human community.

So when we begin to redefine "relationship" in such a way that robots qualify for the job, we need to stop and have a good long careful conversation here. And when our human relationships are increasingly "roboticized" in a sense, cybernated, conducted more and more by on-screen avatars and over pop-up IM windows, we need to have a good long conversation about that, too. Preferably a face-to-face one! Starting a chat room about the inherent limitations of chat-room discourse is just a little too post-modern ironic, don't you think?

It seems to me that the conversation has to start by basic grappling with the question "what does it *mean* to be in relationship?" What is it for? What is the fundamental reality here of relationship? What is friendship? I have over 500 friends on Facebook — but how many of them are truly friends? Could I pick them out of a police lineup (not that my friends are likely to end up in one . . . or are they)? But what does the word mean?

We all experience interiorly the hunger for relationship, for connection, for being-with the other. The "not-good-thing" of being alone is a familiar reality for almost all human beings. Rare is the person who claims to have no need of other people; rare, and frankly, I don't believe him. (It's generally a "him" who would make that claim.) We have emotional needs that clamor for relationship, be it friendship or the more intensely romantic or sexual drive to be-with the other.

Trouble enters into this fundamental human experience when we decide that's what it's all about. In other words, when we determine ourselves to be in a relationship insofar as our emotional needs are being met. So long as I am assuaged in my immediate need for companionship, my relational self is satisfied. This is an understandable way of looking at it, but terrifically problematic.

I can draw an analogy with hunger for food. I have a good appetite, and enjoy few things more than bellying up to the table for a feast. The image of heaven as a wedding banquet speaks deeply to my innermost self, which is a big greedy pig, truth be told.

But my physical hunger pangs can just as easily (more easily, really!) be satisfied by tearing open a large bag of Doritos and scarfing them madly, washing it all down with a Coke. Hunger is satisfied, yes, but my true need is not met. If I subsist on the popular Doritos-Coke diet, terrible things will happen to my body.

The immediate hunger pangs of our emotions and physical appetite for love can equally be met by a robot, an on-line avatar, a pornographic video or a cheap hookup, and we can feel at least for the moment that all is well. The itch, it has been scratched. But are we really in relationship? Are we not still alone in the depths of our being, even if, as Turkle so eloquently puts it, we are alone together? Is there nothing better possible for us than that?

To a narcissist, there is no question. Other

people only exist to meet my emotional needs; that's the point of others, what they are there for. Most of us do not like narcissists.

But if we begin to define human contacts as "human enough" and relationships in such a way that the only relevant point is whether or not my emotional needs are met, have we not conceded the field to narcissism? Have we not fundamentally decided that the narcissistic view of human relationship is the only possible one? We may be nice narcissists who try to meet other people's needs while ours are being met, but narcissists we are nonetheless, if that's the model we live by.

As Doritos and Coke do terrible things to my body, if they are my sole idea of what food is, so does the washed-out, reductionist view of relationship of the narcissist model do terrible things to our humanity. We all have needs; I supply your needs, and you supply mine. These needs, by the way, may have nothing at all to do with sex or romance. But is that all there is? Who are you? Who am I? Do I care about you? Do you care about me? Do we *know* each other? Do we want to?

Narcissism and the failure of human relationship is not exactly a recent phenomenon. After all, Narcissus is a figure of Greek mythology; the Greeks were nothing if not acute observers of human nature. Human beings have been withdrawing from relationship for a long time. I believe it traces back to that unfortunate incident involving a talking snake and a piece of fruit. And, oh, some bushes that the man and woman hid behind. Hid, so as not to be in The Relationship we are made for.

Narcissism and withdrawal are not new, but technology has fashioned a world for us that is all bush, and none of it burning, either. All fig leaf and no true nakedness. You may laugh at my writing that — after all, the Internet is not known as a place devoid of nudity, to put it delicately. But, as Pope John Paul II put it so eloquently, the problem with pornography is not that it exposes too much of the person, but rather too little — in the impersonal and animalistic baring of the physical self, the spiritual self is wholly occluded. I will have more to say about this in the chapter on privacy.

In the pre-technological world, people could withdraw, people could hide behind whatever bushes they found, but it got mighty lonely in there. Today, if I can mix the two metaphors, we can hunker down in the e-bushes scarfing down Doritos and Coke until the day we die. We can keep that technological simulacrum of relationships going merrily along, until we have forgotten what a real relationship looks like. Keep defining it all in terms of "are my needs being met," until the soul-killing disease of narcissism has made any other way of relating impossible.

A world that is all bush, and none of it burning. . . . Of course, the deepest problem here is that we are truly, and in the deepest level of our being, made for friendship, or rather for Friendship. Aquinas defines theological charity as "friendship with God." [12] We are made, not to hide from God behind a bush, but to encounter God amidst all the bushes and brambles of life, and to take off our shoes (even if that means our feet get a little scratched up), for this place of encounter is holy (cf. *Exodus* 3:5). And this friendship with God, this living encounter with Him in which His life becomes ours and ours becomes His — it simply cannot be reduced to a narcissistic exchange.

God has no needs for us to supply. And to put it mildly, He does not exist to fulfill our narcissistic needs. He promises to make us happy, but that's very different from the immediate instant gratification of having every

---

[12] St. Thomas Aquinas, *Summa Theologica*, II.23.1.

itch scratched, every hunger assuaged, every need met now, as I want it.

So the whole question of relationship and its reduction to being "human enough," "relational enough" has to be gone into very seriously, lest we find ourselves utterly unfitted for the very Relationship upon which our eternal happiness rests. There is a banquet table laid for us which will fill us deeply and forever remove the not-good-thing of isolation from our being; but if we spoil our palate by spending our life shovelling in a constant diet of spiritual, emotional and relational junk food, we may find no joy in that banquet. And woe is us, if that is the case. If we cannot befriend God (or rather, accept his eternal friend request), where does that leave us?

Oh, it's all so complicated! It's really all so simple, actually, but because we are not so simple, we find it, we experience it, as a very complex matter, this relationship business. And the deep tendency to simplify it, to withdraw, to reduce it to a sort of economic exchange, to "turn off like a TV" if you let me down, even though that means we are not really in a genuine human relationship: all of that remains with us as a constant struggle.

Technology has changed the terms of this

struggle to some extent. It has made it more endemic, more universal. It has created a world of networks and relational models that positively militate against genuine human relationships, that encourage us to turn each other off like a TV, to withdraw behind masks and avatars, to put on a happy Face(book), pack up your troubles in the old kit bag hidden in the deep recesses of your heart, and smile, smile, smile (though your heart is breaking…). Inauthenticity and superficiality are the hallmarks of on-line relating; the more we live online, the less authentic and truly intimate we are.

It's the "it" factor I referred to earlier. WH Auden, in his Christmas Oratorio *For the Time Being,* describes the night in Bethlehem when "everything was a you and nothing was an it." We are living in an anti-Bethlehem today, where the risk lies in everyone becoming an "it" and nobody being truly a "you." Technology, which is supposed to connect us so efficiently, does indeed connect us, but only on the surface of things.

Of course, the driving force behind this is not technology, nor is it narcissism. It's this whole business of pain, isn't it? None of us likes to be in pain. And intimacy breeds vulnerability. Vulnerability means exposure to injury — and nobody likes being hurt.

True relationship, true encounter of human with human, of human with God, hurts. It hurts on the human level because of the reality of sin, that we betray each other and fail to love each other as we should.

But it also hurts for an even deeper reason. We long for a communion, a unity, a depth of intimacy and understanding and belonging that is total. And this depth of intimacy we desire is precisely what we are simply not going to experience on this earth. There may be fleeting moments where we come very close to it, but, fundamentally, the desire for relationship that we carry in our beings is a desire for heaven. The craving we all have is for the bill of fare being served at that Banquet awaiting us, and nothing else in this life quite satisfies us.

So we have loneliness. We have isolation, that not-good-thing. We have, even in the best relationships, that raw, rude encounter with the limitations of relationships. "He didn't understand me . . . she wasn't there for me . . . I can't believe you let me down — you, of all people!" Deep pain, deep desolation, and it comes to all of us, without exception, if and as we choose to love.

"My God, my God, why have you forsaken me?" It comes to all of us, even as it came to Him. **Relationship, if it is to be not just human enough, but simply human, must consent to be cruciform.** If I choose to love you, sooner or later you will kill me. If you choose to love me, sooner or later I will kill you. Not in a bloody, hammer and nails fashion, probably not intentionally, perhaps against our own best will for one another. It is the nature of the thing.

Even if somehow neither of us does anything to really hurt the other, sooner or later one of us will die, and for the one left, if there was truly love in the relationship, it will be like a dying with that person, except with the added anti-benefit that we will go on breathing and thus hurting. Love leads to death for the lover: it's part of the package. As I said once to one of my spiritual directees: "Two choices: love and tears, or no love and no tears!" She chose love.

So did God. God's choice, in Jesus, to enter and remain in a depth of relationship to us brought Him to tears (*John* 11:35), and then (marvel of marvels!) it killed Him. So this whole business of relationship and our choices around it, and the cost these choices exact of us, is bound up with the deepest realities of life, of faith, of what it means to be human, and what it means to enter the divine sphere.

So we have to tread very carefully here. We have to talk, and think, and maybe even pray about all this business of robot companions for the elderly, online avatars and Facebook "friendships," chatroom etiquette, and the omnipresent "x" on the top right corner of our lives today.

Perhaps we need to twist that x around a bit, those two lines that cross thus, so that they intersect with each other and with us at a somewhat different angle. And placing that reformed x between and before us and each person we encounter on or off line, it will no longer be a sign of our ability to close the window, to withdraw, to reduce each relationship to nothing whenever it gets complicated or a bit bloody. Rather, it can become the Sign and the living reminder marking God's own bloody, simple commitment to relating to us.

A sign that encourages us to make that same choice, plunge into that same complicated messy business of love and relationship, communion and intimacy. The Sign that this, and this alone, is the path leading us to the life we are made for: the life of joy and peace in the communion of heaven.

We need to keep front and center in our relationships that Sign and the One who gave it to us, for it is the Sign of salvation, and eternal life, the life of communion, the Banquet where all our cravings will be at last satisfied. That place where, at last, it is (will be) all good.

Chapter Eight

Becoming a Person

Relationship and all its complex intricate dance in our lives is indeed central to being human. A necessary part of rich human life is, indisputably, the presence of other people in one's universe. "I vant to be alone," Greta Garbo famously said, but of course, her words are remembered only because she said it to *someone.*

Yes, it is crucial to have a true relationship with *someone* to be truly human, but something else comes before this, in importance if not in strict temporal succession. It is this: you have to have a relationship with yourself before you can have the full richness of relationship with the other. There has to be a certain indwelling of the self, a certain interiority of one's own person, before we can really enter the kind of intercommunion we are made for. "Communion" means one-with-ness. If I am not a "one" to begin with, how can I become "one with" you?

Now this inner integration, this becoming a "one" so as to be able to be with the other, admittedly happens in a wide variety of ways. It's a complex process, perhaps requiring the whole of a person's life to be completed.

It begins in the womb, as we are knit together in the hidden darkness of the body of our mother. Who can say what happens in the interiority of the person in those first nine months?

Upon emerging from that hidden place, we become involved in all the human realities we all know about: the love and affirmation of parents and others, the processes of education and individuation that make up a healthy childhood, the hard lessons and inevitable mistakes of adolescence and early adulthood, the taking on of responsibility and adult commitments that should follow upon these, and so on, to the full flowering of that most marvelous of creatures, a mature human person.

But all of this, even if it is all well in place, is gravely impeded if one crucial ingredient is missing in the human experience. There is one thing every human being needs if all the formation and education and experiential richness of life is to become integrated and interiorized in the developing person.

We need silence. Silence is that dark hidden place, the womb of our humanity, the place where all the formative elements of our humanity are knit together into a whole. It is the place where we become a person.

We live in a world of noise. This is not a new situation, exactly, even if it has grown somewhat louder in recent decades. There is always input, stimulus, information and exhortation coming at us from multiple directions. And this input is necessary to our formation as human beings. We are not isolated monads.

But all this information needs to be incorporated, integrated, processed, digested. Otherwise, it lies fallow, remaining at the level of mere random stimuli striking our sensory nerves. It is in silence that we perform this process of taking all the world gives us and making it our own, fitting it, sorting it, analyzing it, rejecting it, perhaps, but at any rate allowing that information to become part of our emerging person.

Silence — this is something I know a lot about. I mentioned in the last chapter that being a member of Madonna House qualifies me as a relationship expert of sorts, if not in the talk-radio, Oprah-esque sense of the word.

It also qualifies me as a sort of "silence expert" (tacitologist? sigeologist? hush puppy?). I have spent most of my years in MH living in our main headquarters buried deep in the Upper Ottawa Valley of Ontario, Canada. We live in the wilderness. Traffic is sparse (we joke that more than three cars converging on a single stretch of the road is "rush hour gridlock"). Nature is quiet, especially in the long winter months. There is no heavy industry, no police sirens, really just not all that many people out here.

And in the community itself, there is little to no media noise. No radios blaring, no TV, no blasting away of music into ear buds, no constant stream of information and entertainment coming at us through a half dozen technological portals. At least we're not being barraged as a normal state of affairs, anyhow. We have all those devices (we're not Amish!) but we choose to pass our days in as much silence and recollection as our given work allows. We generally don't even chit chat too much as we go about the work of the day.

Many of us, myself included, go once a

week or so for an even more intense experience of silence as we spend a day in
poustinia. This is a Russian word meaning
"desert," which in the Christian spiritual tradition is the place of silence, prayer,
encounter with God and with oneself in a
certain emptiness of space and time. In
poustinia one has the Bible to read, and
bread and water for food. The room or cabin
is deliberately Spartan in its furnishings: bed,
chair, desk, cross. No decorations or frilly
bits and pieces. Maybe an icon on the wall
with a vigil light burning before it. But stark,
empty, and very, very silent.

All of which is to say we who live this
way day in and day out know a great deal
about silence, its challenges, and its fruitfulness. And this fruitfulness is tangible. People
who come to spend time at MH often remark
at what a bunch of strong individuals the
members of the community are. The only
cookie cutters in use at MH are used (actually) to cut cookies. We are indeed a wild
bunch of random oddballs, hugely different
from one another in temperament, interests,
opinions, talent and lack thereof. Deeply
united in Catholic faith and an essential vision of life, we are otherwise really a bunch

of flaming individualists.

I hold that it is the very silence and austerity of our community environment that produces this strength of character and individual identity among us. There is input in all of our lives. MH is not a Carthusian monastery living in grand silence most of the day. We have our noise, too. But the conscious choice towards silence means that we can absorb the noise of life, the words filling our common space, the clatter and clash of the world as it beats in on us, and integrate it into our own personal being.

Silence is emptiness of sorts, by definition. It is absence: of noise, of words. There is a certain poverty that is entailed here. If words/noise/input are "wealth," or at least fullness, then in silence we enter a sort of personal poverty, an empty space, a place which is not being filled from outside. And from this emptiness, this poverty, out of this "desert" emerges . . . well, me.

Or, you. Or, whoever. What do I really think? What am I really feeling? What is going on in the real me, under all the barrage of noise and words and impressions and sensory stimuli of my day? Only in silence can the real Fr. Denis Lemieux emerge from the wreckage, so to speak, of the daily noise-tsunami.

My own experience in poustinia is just that: when I go into poustinia, generally the first few hours are spent with all the words and noise and input of the previous week raging and rattling and echoing within me and finally sputtering out into quiet . . . and out of that quiet, what is really happening within my heart and soul begins to take shape. I begin to shape a word that is my own true word out of the silence I find there. Necessity is the mother of invention; poverty and emptiness are the mother of authenticity, personal honesty, integrity.

Now, it is just possible that someone reading this may be violently objecting at this point, "Well, that's all well and good for you! You live in the wilderness! You live in a religious community! You can have the luxury of quiet and silence and days in poustinia! Lucky you! I've got twelve kids all under the age of five! I'm working 170-hour workweeks! I'm living under an over-pass in the Bronx, me and my twelve kids! What about me!?"

Perhaps I exaggerate your circumstances a bit. Perhaps you wouldn't necessarily end every sentence with an exclamation point. Well, it is true that MH is a place of a more intense silence than perhaps most people could attain (although I do refer you back to the previous chapter where there are 200 of us living together here. It ain't all poustinia, in other words).

But we do all have choices, you know. Is there a TV in your house (or under the overpass)? Is it on much? Is the radio on much? How many movies do you watch? How much Internet consumption? Just how often do you have those little ear buds sprouting from your ears? And is there a man with a gun living in your house forcing you to keep all these devices on so much? We have choices, you know.

I remember those Hulu ads from a couple years back, the ones with the very funny if sadly intemperate Alec Baldwin playing an alien launching the online TV site as "an evil plot to destroy your minds..." since, after all, "you can't turn all your devices off at once!" The commercials were funny, admittedly, but also audacious in their up-front admission of the bad impact of their product — a classic example of the marketing principle of turning a negative into a positive (another notable example of the principle: "With a name like Smuckers, it has to be good!").

Because we can in fact turn off all our devices at once. And to have a constant blaring of TV shows, pop songs, internet chatter, YouTube videos coming at you hour after hour after hour . . . well, all melodrama aside, it does destroy your mind.

It's like the scene in *A Clockwork Orange* where they strap the juvenile delinquent Alex into a chair with his eyeballs forced open and make him watch movies for hour upon hour so as to program him to react in certain automatic ways, in order to render him incapable of violence. Except we've strapped ourselves into the chair. We've signed ourselves up to become clockwork oranges because . . . Well, I guess because it's easier than becoming a person.

There are times in our lives when silence is elusive, granted. But even in those busy years, we have choices. I remember visiting a home-schooling mother with eight or nine kids ranging from early teens down to a baby. She wanted to have a little visit with me and to enjoy that rarest of commodities for her, namely a sustained conversation with another adult, so she flatly informed her children,

"It's reading time!" Off they all went with their respective books (coloring books for the little ones) to their rooms. The baby was napping, and blessed silence reigned. . . .

Another stay-at-home mom, this one with five kids on the younger end of the scale was lamenting to me the lack of silence in the home. I told her to incorporate into their morning prayers before the school day began a period of silent prayer together. She tried it, and her kids loved it. To just sit together in silent, listening prayer for a few minutes! Children have a considerable capacity for silence, you know, until it is squeezed out of them by media overload and hyper-stimulus.

So, technology. We all know, I think, that this technological world is a noisy, noisy, noisy one. Whether it's the explicit noise of music and TV and movies or the more subtle "silent noise" of constant verbal input: texts and tweets, blogs and updates and IMs, we are in a state (if we choose) of constant sensory bombardment, a constant taking in of information or at least data (much of what splashes around on the internet can only be formally recognized as "information").

But the consequences of this sensory overload are poorly understood, I believe.

The social cost of raising a generation who have done very little if any of this "sitting together in silence," very little of this interior poustinia, this inner encounter with self away from noise — do we appreciate it? The young people coming to MH in the last five to ten years find it increasingly difficult to enter into the silence of our way of life. They get bored. They get antsy. They need their tunes, their games, their movies. If they can stick it out for the first few weeks, something good happens, but the initial entry is increasingly difficult. This bears witness to a profound interior impoverishment in our society.

To what degree are we not really thinking our own thoughts, not really coming up with our own views, feelings, true responses to reality? To what degree do we simply parrot clichés and catch phrases, the latest memes coming out of the hive mind of the cyberworld? To what extent, more subtly, is our very train of thought dictated by the movement of the currents of debate and discussion? How much do we allow the very terms and flow of such debate to be set by others rather than by what we truly believe to be the essence of the matter?

For example, I have long ago removed the words "conservative" and "liberal" from my own interior vocabulary, and I try to avoid using them in discussions with people. I consider them meaningless, and hence valueless terms. In particular, I consider them odious and destructive in terms of religious discussions. I expressed my thoughts on that matter once to a fellow seminarian. He was utterly flummoxed and could only stammer at me, "But . . . those are the words everyone uses!"

It is only in silence and separation, in unhooking and unplugging, in entering into that strange emptiness and poverty, that we are liberated from the words "everyone uses," that we can come to our true selves, our own words and ideas, that we are able to sort out what is rubbish from what is truth, what is mere conformity and convention from what is truly ours. To be free from what Chesterton called "the most degrading slavery to the spirit of the age" — this requires, in our day more than ever, silence.

It is a question of interior freedom, which is threatened at this precise moment in 2013 in North America, not so much by explicit government coercion or curtailing of human rights (although serious issues exist in this field, the denial of the right to life to unborn human beings by far the most grave), but by the incessant shaping of our perception of reality by non-stop consumption of media.

The original meaning of the word "glamour" is relevant here: before being concerned mostly with hair, makeup, and clothing, it first referred to a type of magical spell used to distort the vision of the enchanted one (in Harry Potterese, "Estée Lauderus!"). We are a glamorized society: what we see is all too often a product of packaging and cropping, spin doctoring and outright lies. Silence, the retreat into the poustinia of the heart, is of the essence in unenchanting ourselves so as to see more clearly.

Out of this unenchantment, we can then issue forth with the second fruit of silence. **The first fruit of silence is becoming a true person; the second fruit of silence is having something to say.** In other words, creativity. To have something to contribute, something of one's own to bring forth to the table of man, to be something of an original, a unique figure, a "character" — this is the business of creativity, and it is born from the womb of silence. If all we have resonating in our heads is the words, music, pictures, and thoughts of others, how will we ever have anything of our own to give?

"You have to be somebody before you can share yourself,"[13] says Jaron Lanier in his thought provoking critique of current Internet culture. Without the hard work of becoming a somebody, all we are left with, as he points out quite trenchantly, is constant retreads and rehashes: mashups, samplings, re-makes, retro . . . in other words, about 95% of current popular culture these days.

There is a third fruit of silence in our lives. Those discerning readers who have noticed that I am a Catholic priest may wonder that I've taken this long to get around to it. That I have is not because it is least important or tangential. Far from it — without this final fruit, the other fruits ultimately wither on the vine, too.

My reason for leaving it to the end is simple and rhetorical. Everyone wants to be a person; most people want some kind of creativity in their lives; it is only a smaller number who explicitly, consciously desire God.

---

[13] Jaron Lanier, *You Are Not a Gadget: A Manifesto,* (New York: Random House, 2011), p. xiii.

And **this is where we meet God: in silence, in recollection**. You know, I don't actually go to poustinia to meet myself or think my own thoughts. I go there to pray. In MH, we choose to live a relatively silent life, as circumstances permit, not simply so we can all become strong individuals (that's a by-product, really), but because we are trying to listen to God and live in His presence in the midst of our busy days.

It is in this aspect that silence truly deepens and broadens to become something much bigger, much more beautiful, much more all-encompassing than can be treated in a book about technology and its misuse. When we come to be aware that within the silence of this day, this moment, there is Another present with us, when we come to know that being human is not simply being in relationship with one another but with this Very Other, this mysterious One, this . . . God, whatever that word really means (the further one dwells and delves into it, the more deeply mysterious it all gets, you know) — well silence becomes a little bit more than just a place for us to cool off and process life. It becomes the very place where we are, in the words of Paul Evdokimov, "mysteriously visited" by . . . Him. The One our hearts long for.

Technology, if its use is out of control, robs us of all this. It robs us of ourselves, robs us of our creativity, and robs us of a living connection with God. The world has gotten noisier and noisier with each passing decade of the last 200 years. And atheism and religious indifference have grown, it seems, with each passing decade as well. While correlation does not equal causality, the question does arise: are we drowning out the voice of God? And, is this a good thing to do? What voice is taking its place? A voice that loves us? That tells us the truth? Or is it the harsh clamorous voice of the mob, the flashy "glamorous" voice of the rich and powerful, the positive forceful voice of the opinion shapers, the manipulators, the ones who seek to manage us into submission, into being good little clockwork oranges programmed to react in "this" way to "that" stimulus?

Only in silence can we come to ourselves. Only in silence can we come to the One who made us. And only in silence with ourselves and He Who made us, can our being be knit together in truth and in peace. **Only in**

silence can our own words, blending with the Word, take shape in us, take flesh in us, so that we become real persons.

God became a man in silence, in that mysterious virginal womb; we, in the womb of silence, recollection, and love, become not just men and women in authenticity and integrity, but men and women filled with the life and Spirit of God with and within us.

It is necessary. There is no other way

.

Chapter Nine

Look at Me!

T*IME Magazine* had a cover story on Facebook a couple of years ago. The headline was "How Facebook is redefining privacy, and what this means for you." This headline struck me forcibly. It had an extraordinary degree of anti-genius, one at which one can only marvel. To write something that stupid is not easy; years of training and a native incapacity for thought are required, I suspect.

The headline captured in a few words the whole approach to reality I am combating in this book. Namely, the sense that technology and its various component parts (e.g., Facebook) are inevitably and willfully changing everything around us, that we have absolutely no say in the matter, and our only option is to capitulate and adjust our expectations and behaviors accordingly.

Note to *TIME* and to Mark Zuckerburg, Google, Microsoft and Apple: Facebook and all other technological platforms and products do not and never will "define" anything about me or about anyone else unless and until we choose to allow it that privilege. If you beg to differ, all I can say is, "Bring it on, baby! Let's rumble!!"

The headline also brings us to another element of our humanity we need to talk about. Privacy: what is this word? What does it mean? Why does it matter? What good does it do? Does it still exist? Can it? Does anyone care about it? Should they? (And, can I stop turning every sentence I write into a question? Well, can I? Who knows? Do you?)

It seems to me that the business of privacy is in fact precisely the place where the previous two chapters of this book meet. The question of authentic human relationships and the question of silence and personal authenticity are bound together in this whole question of privacy.

In silence, we become truly ourselves; in relationship, we are truly with the other. In a proper and ordered sense of privacy, we see in action the virtue by which we control our true self-revelation, our true self-disclosure, so that the relationships we enter into are true and real.

This is the virtue of discretion, which also flows from that central human good discussed back in Chapter Two, the exercise of intellect and free will. We are to exercise a rationally understood and free control of our own self-disclosure. The growth of relationship from the most casual of acquaintances towards the depths of intimacy of man and woman in marriage and all the stages of friendship and love in between is meant to be an ordered one. So we have to have some understanding here (intellect!) and some self-control (will power!).

This used to be so abundantly clear that it didn't need to be talked about. A mere fifty years ago, everyone knew that there were such things as family matters, not to be discussed openly at large, that there were other subjects that could be confided to one's closest friends, and other subjects that were matters of general knowledge and conversation. There was a certain amount of leeway and slack in the system, and the precise boundaries certainly varied from place to place and family to family, but the basic concept was universally understood and agreed upon.

Some would argue that this was not wholly a good thing; that all sorts of abuse could be hidden behind closed doors, disguised as a private family matter for example. This cannot be denied. But this is hardly our problem today. Today, the good of privacy is increasingly forgotten, ignored, outright denied. Wikileaks founder Julian Assange explicitly denies the legitimacy of privacy. Paul McMullan, a reporter involved in the 2011 phone tapping scandal in the UK, called privacy nothing but a cover under which people can do evil ("Privacy is for paedos," was the money quote). Eric Schmidt, the CEO of Google said in a 2009 interview that if you are doing anything you don't want the whole world to know about, you probably shouldn't be doing it.

In other words, privacy is today increasingly identified as an evil thing; the total exposure of all deeds to the light of publicity is seen as good and healthy. And many would ask, so what? What is wrong with this picture? What's the problem?

To answer a question with a question, why do we wear clothes? Aside from the risk of frostbite in painful places, that is. Why do we wear clothes indoors or in warm weather? Nobody considers the body to be evil any more, and I don't think that was ever a widely held view, honestly. But no matter how we feel about our bodies or how objectively perfect or somewhat less than that they might be, we all cover up nonetheless.

The problem is not with our bodies, really. The problem is with our souls. My body is good, a beloved creature of God, a temple of the Holy Spirit. You, gazing upon it in its naked glory, may however not come to that conclusion, quite. (I'm kind of a paunchy, saggy middle-aged man, to be painfully frank.)

On the other end of the scale, the body of a beautiful woman or man may possess all the perfection of the human form we could aspire to, but the soul of the one beholding that body is prone to look upon it as an object for use, a means of self-gratification, something to be possessed. An object of lust, to put it bluntly.

In other words, we cover our bodies up not because they are vile and evil, but because they are too good, too precious to be exposed to the eyes and hearts of sinful humanity. And a similar dynamic is at play around questions of privacy.

There are events in the history of the Lemieux family that I will not consign to paper in this or any book. It is not because of any shame or evil, necessarily. It is because you, my reader, do not know me or my family. If I recount to you mere facts and events, dates and places of my private family history, you will be tempted, perhaps, to judge, to criticize, or to rashly think you know more about me and my family than you do. So, to protect you from that lamentable state of soul, and to protect myself and my family from the pitiless glare of public exposure, there are certain things I will never write about. They are, frankly, none of your business.

So now I have everyone's curiosity well piqued. Too bad for you! But that's the point: curiosity is not a virtue. To want to know about things that are no concern of yours is a vice.

For example, Charlie Sheen is indisputably a mentally ill sex-and-drug addict, or at least that was the case in the year 2011, when his words and deeds became a big media story. Everyone knows that.

But why do I need to know about that? Why do you need to know that? Yes, we can pray for him, but we cannot seriously claim that to have been the motivation behind the media feeding frenzy that surrounded that poor sick man. And we can multiply Sheen by several hundreds if not thousands of celebrities whose private tragedies have become tabloid fodder for the entertainment of the masses. This is shameful, and the fact that we are used to it and find it unremarkable is more shameful yet.

At the Last Judgment, at the final summing up of the books of creation, all will be exposed, all brought to the light. But the light in which everything will be illuminated will be the light of the Divine Charity, the light of mercy and tenderness. In heaven, there are no private matters; but in heaven, there is also nothing but love, God's love eternally poured forth upon all the redeemed, God's love flowing through each one of them to all. Only in that purified state of being, only with those eyes and hearts purified by mercy received and mercy given can we confidently and gladly accept an end to privacy.

This is not the state of affairs now. So I will keep my private affairs private because you do not love me as you should. You may keep your private affairs private because I do not love you as I should. That's the essential point in all this, the good of privacy, of discretion. It is a question of human dignity and proper love of self and neighbour in a fallen world.

And if on occasion things are kept private which should be exposed, if harm is done in secret and not put a stop to quickly enough — well, the hyper-exposed world in which we are all living has not exactly put an end to abuse and violence, in case you haven't noticed. It has only robbed us of our dignity and made us into peeping Toms of one another's lives. Abusers will find ways of keeping their abuse under cover, no matter what.

But there is another aspect of privacy that is not quite covered by what I have written so far in this chapter. We have established (I hope) that privacy has a point, a value, a purpose. That it protects all of us from the loveless gaze of sinful humanity, and from the temptation to that curiosity which is the thirst for knowledge without love.

But the fact remains that it is increasingly normal for people to eagerly put their most intimate personal lives out there in the open for all to see, in the public square. People post on Facebook the most intimate details of their sexual lives, the ins and outs of their relationships, their inmost thoughts and feelings. It is hard to speak of invading the privacy of others when those others are in fact the ones doing the invading, sharing indiscriminately and at top volume the most personal details of their lives.

In other words, we are volunteers, mostly, not victims. What is this strange compulsion that seizes people to put their private business out there for the world to see? Not to be crude, but they put their private parts out there, as well. "Sexting" and the like: why would anyone do this?

The answer, I think, lies in a terrible need: the need to be seen, to be acknowledged, to have someone call you by your name, to recognize you. Simply, the need to be known. This is a profound need of the human person.

And so we put ourselves on exhibit. We get loud, we try to attract attention. Some are better at it than others, some feel this need more than others, but there is a deep desire in us to be known, to be recognized, to have our value and our being affirmed.

And so, as the culture gets louder, we get louder. As people begin to clamor more deeply for this attention, for the "fifteen minutes of fame," everyone has to up their game.

Young girls wear less and less clothing. They begin to style their hair and slather on the makeup at younger and younger ages. Everything is about being "hot," about attracting for at least a moment that look of appreciation. To be an object of desire, to someone, somewhere.

And people begin to reveal more and more outrageous things, speak more wildly, take more and more extreme positions, just to be the center of the discussion however briefly. And so it goes in a cyclone of increasing intensity. People yell out intimate details of their lives; others try to top each other by saying more and more outrageous/vulgar/bizarre things; others take off their clothes, engage publicly in sexual acts of increasing perversity and vileness.

All of it is a constant clamor that says one thing and one thing only. "Look at me, look at me, look at me, look at me!!! Please, won't someone look at me?" The desperate desire, the desperate need for attention, is for someone to know me, to choose me, to love me. And it is tragic: as we shed our clothes, our inhibitions, our morals, any sense of decency or charity or real beauty, we are not known at all. We make an exhibition of ourselves, and the result is a deeper isolation, a deeper loneliness.

Once someone has taken off his or her clothes and posted the pictures on the internet, what is left to reveal? Nothing, and everything. The person remains hidden, lost really, while they seemingly bare all and tell all to the whole world. I know Charlie Sheen is a mentally ill sex-and-drug addict, but I do not know Charlie Sheen, not at all. Not one little bit, even as he has willingly exposed so much of his inner demons to the gaze of the world.

All of this bears witness to a profound spiritual poverty, a spiritual hunger that is unassuaged. For a Christian, there is no question here. Our desire to be known, to be seen, to be affirmed and loved, real as it is, is met constantly and continually by God Who, being God, is able to see, know, and love every one of His creatures in a perfect and abiding way.

And it is the life of prayer that holds this truth before us and constantly enables us to access it. Prayer is the place where we pour out our hearts, the most intimate thoughts and hopes and dreams and secrets, the most shameful failures, the most heartfelt sentiments to this One Who hears, sees, knows, loves.

And prayer is where we are met, somehow, mysteriously, in a way no one who prays can describe adequately. We are known there. The compulsion to scream out all these private matters into the ether of cyberspace bespeaks a profound loss of interiority and spiritual life in the world today.

And of course **these two failures of privacy, voyeurism and exhibitionism, are interwoven.** If someone has exposed himself in public, then he must prod and probe until the other person is as exposed as well. When we are all shameless, then there is no more shame. When they see the media spotlight shine with such intense focus on those celebrities who make exhibitionist spectacles of themselves, young people conclude that that's the way to do it: if you want attention, you had better cue the music and start the striptease. "You gotta get a gimmick, if you wanna get a hand," as the song from *Gypsy* goes.

It is all so tragically unnecessary, and what is lost in all of it is so precious and vital to our human thriving and our dignity. The whole concept of the self as a treasure to be cherished, the elegant and dignified dance by which we slowly entrust the other with this treasure as a relationship begins and deepens, the clear and firm understanding of what there is in my life that is for the whole world to know, what is for my general friends and social circle to know, what is for my close friends and family to know, what is for my spouse to know, and what finally is for God and God alone to know: all of this is lost today, especially for young people growing up in this culture.

This being lost, so much else is lost. True and authentic relationships are lost; if I have bared my soul to the Internet, what do I have left that's just for you? Interiority, silence, the interior castle is lost: how can God come to the innermost recesses of my being to give me Himself if those interior recesses have been scattered to the four winds of the cybersphere?

So much is lost . . . and the world created by this hyper-exposed culture is not a world human beings can live in. The constant baring of secrets and flesh, the trumpeting of one another's sins and failures in the constant din of the chattering classes, the free-for-all of information where anything and everything can be and is blared aloud to the whole world: all of this is a Final Judgment without mercy, without wisdom, without God. And this is unbearable. Something will have to change here, and if that change needs to start here and now with you and me, well, why not?

Many people shrug all this off and say, "Well, what can you do? It's just the way the world is now." No. It is not simply the way the world is now. It is the way we have made the world.

We *are* the world. And we can make the world different if we choose. We can choose to turn away from inappropriate exhibitions of private matters in public. We can choose to regain our own proper boundaries, our own sense of privacy and what things should not be discussed in public, let alone posted on the internet for the world to see.

We don't have to go back to the Victorian era, when proper ladies could say that their names only appeared in the newspapers three times: at their birth, their wedding, and their death. But we can divorce ourselves from the ideal of publicity, the cultural sense that what really counts in life is making a splash, getting the headlines, the buzz.

For the Victorian ladies, what really counted was good breeding and aristocratic bearing. For us, what really counts is loving and being loved, knowing ourselves to be known and loved by God and giving ourselves over to the task of love in the world. From this, all else falls into place. Without this, we flail around trying to get what we need where it isn't, and doing whatever it takes to get it. And that's what's really going on under the surface with all this business of privacy.

It's not a question of Facebook and what it is doing or not doing to us. It's a question of where your face and my face are turned. What is our life about, anyhow? When we know that, we will know where and how to give ourselves, spend ourselves, and entrust ourselves to God and to others in an ordered and beautiful way.

Chapter Ten

Driving to Toronto

Well, what is it all about anyway? You know my answer. I outlined it back in Chapter Three. You may agree with that answer, or you may have a very different one. Or maybe you don't know. But what's it about? Life, that is. Your life, my life, the life of the world? Is it about anything? Is it all pointless? Do our actions, our choices ultimately mean anything, or is it all an ultimately futile exercise? You live, stuff happens, and then you die. The end. Is that it? Or is there a meaning to it all?

My final reflection on technology and humanity is that **human life is *consequential*.** So if you disagree, and subscribe to the above view of life as ultimately meaningless, you can skip this chapter (actually, you can skip the whole book, but for some strange reason you appear to have made it this far, so you may as well hang in for the last bit).

Human life is consequential. It is going somewhere. It has a point, a purpose, an end. If this is true, then everything in our life is either this end, or it is a means to this end, or it is a distraction from this end. This seems to me to be a rigorous logical argument. If I'm driving to Toronto, everything on that drive is either Toronto itself, a road that takes me to Toronto, or a detour.

Now, I may rightly choose to take that detour, for various reasons. For example, from where I live the precise direct route to Toronto takes me through the smaller city of Peterborough. There is a detour that skirts around Peterborough, so as to avoid having to drive through it. It's longer, but ultimately faster. Or I might stop off on the way to visit some friends nearby, or for a bite to eat. That there are detours on the way to Toronto that I can rightly choose is possible because, of course, going to Toronto is not (thank you, Jesus) my final end, the end-in-itself of my life, but is merely one small end that fits into my whole life made up of a host of other means and ends.

But is there in fact an end-in-itself to our life as a whole? Is there an end for which our whole being is made, our whole life directed? Is there a final point to existence, towards which our whole being is meant to be directed? If there is not, then human life is a pretty tragic affair, don't you think? We go here, we go there, we go to Toronto for some strange reason, we get married, we have children . . . all good ends. But without some final end to our life, some final purpose that all this fits into, what are we left with?

A rotting corpse, that's what. And even if we have children, and they have children, and that seems to extend our being into some greater purpose . . . well, not to be cruel, but they're all going to end up as rotten corpses, too. And if our lives are supposed to have some deeper meaning within the large project of the world, of the universe in some fashion or other . . . well, sorry, but there again the whole physical universe is ultimately heading towards being a rotten corpse, too. And, anyhow, why should little me with my little lifespan really care about the fate of the universe, if I'm only present in it for 100 years, maximum? So I'm a link in a chain . . . but if the whole chain is rusting and eroding and about to fall apart and isn't attached to anything anyhow, what good is it my being a link? A useless link in a useless chain — bah!

If the whole thing isn't going somewhere, we are indeed tragic figures, playing out our little dramas on a shabby stage that all too soon opens up a trap door under our feet plunging us down into an abyss of meaninglessness.

> Tomorrow, and tomorrow, and tomorrow,
> Creeps in this petty pace from day to day,
> ...
> Life's but . . . a tale
> Told by an idiot, full of sound and fury,
> Signifying nothing.[14]

Shakespeare pretty much nailed it — nihilism is not a modern invention.

Now, I don't believe any of that for a minute and never have, so I can contemplate this stark ugly picture with a fair amount of equanimity. I believe that life is meaningful, that there is a final purpose, and that this final purpose is meant (as final purposes always are) to shape every little bit of my life here and now.

We are meant to live intentional, thoughtful, decisive, purposeful lives. God and our communion with Him is the only true and absolute end to our lives, because He is the only good in our life that is strong enough to endure forever, to carry us over

---

[14] *Macbeth,* Act 5, Scene 5.

the threshold of death and decay into some mysterious mode of life that is everlasting, that makes our life not futile, not pointless, but extremely, beautifully meaningful.

It is a matter of strict logic that if God is the ultimate end of our life, everything else in greater or lesser degrees is meant to be a means to this divine end. It is not like going to Toronto, which is one partial end in competition with other ends (e.g., visiting friends, avoiding city traffic, eating). That which is The End to life admits of no detours, no side trips, no stops along the way. Our whole life is meant to be shaped, fashioned to its intentional end. There is no other end to which one particle of my time can rightly be given, if we understand properly what is meant by the word "end" and its all-encompassing implications.

"Life is real, life is earnest, and the grave is not the goal!"[15] So one of the wise elders of Madonna House used to quote to me from time to time. Of course this can sound rather grim, if we don't understand it properly. Everything in my life is about God and my communion with Him, so I better be on my

---

[15] Henry Wadsworth Longfellow, "A Psalm of Life."

knees praying the rosary all day. Better not pay attention to anything or anyone except God, ever. Better not relax, ever.

That would be a pretty ugly picture, and if that were true, perhaps it would be better to forget about our higher purpose and, indeed, just have some fun and do the best we can. There will always be time (so we think) when we get older and can't kick up our heels the way we used to, and then we will give some thought to eternity and God and religion and all that stuff.

But that's not the ugly picture of life. This God, at least the God the Catholic Church has taught me to believe in and worship, is a God Who loves every created thing He made, and most especially every person He made. So my intentional, earnest life directed at every waking moment towards my communion with Him (well, at least I *wish* my every waking moment was so directed) is therefore directed towards loving all His creatures the way He loves them.

To delight in the world God made and all that fills it, to look on every human being as a marvelous creature of God, marred and broken a bit, yes, by sin, but nonetheless bearing the mark of the Master Craftsman in his being, to always and everywhere be seeking to regard and embrace all creatures of God exactly as He regards and embraces them, this is the intentional Christian life in the world.

Even at the moments that may seem the most carefree, the most uninhibited and abandoned, even when we're having fun, joking around, having a party, it's because we *intend* to have a party and joke and have fun. Having fun and laughing together builds family, builds relationship.

Celebration is really important in living a godly life in the world. Celebrating is a way of saying that life and the world are good things; ultimately, to celebrate, to be zany and carefree and goofy is an act of worship, of rendering to God the due acknowledgement that He has made a good world, full of things to delight in, to laugh about, to rejoice over.

Celebrating, playing games, having fun, is also a pious act whereby we acknowledge that the care of the whole world does not rest on our feeble frames: there is a God in heaven watching over us who loves us. So we can laugh a little, joke a little, hoist a glass or two together, play a game together. It is no trivial pursuit, nor is it balderdash to do so. Indeed, get a clue: we incur a great deal of risk if we scrabble about trying to take control of the world, as if we have a monopoly on taking responsibility for it. (Note to editor: is my prose here a bit sub-par? Cheesy? That's life -- sorry!) Relax and roll the dice, is what I'm saying. Or, as another of our wise elders at MH used to say, "Shut up and deal!" It's a spiritual exercise.

But, in all these matters, we're meant to be in control of our choices and movements. We are meant to be mindful of what we are doing and why, what our life is about and how this action we are doing is at the service of God, of communion, of love, of the final goal and point of all reality. And, with that vision always somewhere operative in our being, to do whatever we do for a reason that is good and true.

Now, technology can absolutely be used in a consequential way. No question of that. We can use technology to communicate with people far away on the other side of the world, through Skype or e-mail or Facebook. And our communication will be filled with whatever we have in our hearts for those people: love and concern, or other things that may not be so good and true.

Technology can be used to disseminate truth to the four corners of the globe in the time it takes me to type this sentence. It can be used to make works of beauty available to the masses, and to mobilize millions of people in some concerted good effort: think of the organized charitable responses to natural disasters like the tsunami in Indonesia or the earthquake in Haiti. Technology is morally neutral, simply extending the power of our actions to achieve more than our unaided human efforts can accomplish.

Modern information technology can also be a shiny toy that distracts and diverts us in an unlimited fashion. The ultimate detour on the road of life, it can pull us away from our purpose and goal into hours and hours of surfing the net to find out the latest celebrity gossip or the latest buzz or watch the latest viral YouTube video, or, or, or...

This is hardly a new phenomenon. Gossip is as old as the Garden of Eden (so, Eve, I heard that God told you not to eat the fruits in the garden! Is that true? Come on, girl-friend, dish the dirt!). Diversions and distractions have always been with us, and indeed recreation itself has a proper place in a divinely ordered life, being a facet of proper self-love and self-care.

What is new (relatively) is that we have these little boxes or tablets in our homes that can take us to every corner of the globe at any moment at the touch of a screen, that can fill hours and hours of time with just about anything we want: good, bad, or neutral, in a literally endless flow of information and amusement.

There is simply more information out there and coming into our little boxes and tablets at us than we can absorb. It is a bit of an inversion of what we have been taught about heaven, where our whole being is filled to overflowing with the transforming and unutterably beautiful vision of God. Here, instead of God, our beings are filled to overflowing with our own self-directed absorption of data, words, images streaming through our consciousness in every waking hour with . . . what? With anything worthwhile? Anything that helps us get to where we are going?

It is very shiny and loud and endlessly varying, and it can have a real hypnotic effect in our life. And we have to be watchful of that. Where is it taking you? Is this video, this website, this chat room, a means to an end? To what end? A good end? God? Is it helping you to love? If not, why are you there?

Consequence: this is essential to a human life. Animals just go from thing to thing, guided by instinctual responses and their basic animal desires. There is no great consequence to the life of a rabbit. They do, indeed, get born, live, do stuff, and then die. Goodbye, bunny! And if we want to live and die like rabbits, we can do so.

If we want to live and die, and live again like human beings caught up in the mystery of God and love, we have to live differently from our beloved animal friends. Live as if it all means something, and shape our responses, our choices according to what it all means. Far from being a grim, joyless way of life, this is a life bursting with enthusiasm, energy, zeal, and (really!) lots and lots of fun.

When we know that it's all for something, that everything, every moment, every day, everything around us is bearing us somewhere, and that this somewhere is Really Good, then we can throw ourselves into life, like a swimmer throwing himself into the ocean's surf; joyful abandon as we take on each day with purpose and vigour, knowing that all of it together is held and shaped and fashioned by One Who loves us and Who wants our life to be shaped into His life.

Or we can waste our time on trivialities and amusements and diversions; it's our choice, I guess. But if we do that, how will we ever get to "Toronto?" How will we ever get to where we're trying to go?

Chapter Eleven

Conclusion

I was talking to Kaylee, the Madonna House dog, the other day, and told her I was working on this book called *The I-Choice: Staying Human in a Digital Age.* She got very excited upon hearing that, jumping up on me and barking and wiggling her butt as dogs do when they are excited. When she calmed down, she told me why. It turns out that she herself is working on a book right now in response to the increasing cat population in the neighborhood. She is calling it *The Dog-Choice: Staying Canine in a Feline Age.* Amazing coincidence, eh?

Then I went up to our St. Benedict's Acres, our community's farm and had a cozy tête-à-tête with Daisy the horse. She was anguishing about her equine identity on a farm with a large herd of cows. She had recently foaled and was distressed: "How will I raise little Noel to not become bovine?" she neighed at me. Meanwhile the cows were having their weekly book club, and were animatedly discussing their latest selection: *Don't Have a Cow, Man — Be a Cow! A Celebration of All Things Bovine.*

Now of course, none of these things actually happened, and not just because of the whole lamentable non-talking/reading/ writing thing with animals. Even if they could read, write, and talk, they wouldn't talk like that.

Have you ever noticed that animals do not have existential crises? They just don't. Even the most intelligent animal species, even chimpanzees and dolphins, seem just fine being exactly what they are. Pigs is pigs, the world round.

It is not so with us. Indeed, perhaps the most distinctive characteristic of human beings in the world, the hallmark of being human, is that we have to choose it. We have to struggle to remain human and to grow to the fullness of our humanity. We have to protest and fight against dehumanization, against the fragmenting of our being, the degradation of our dignity, the destruction of our identity.

The phrase sometimes used about this or that behavior is "well, that's what keeps us human!" What really keeps us human is that we and we alone have occasion to use that phrase. That there is something to be kept, something that can be lost or destroyed, something we have to struggle to maintain: this makes us unique among all creatures.

There is nothing new about the struggle to stay human. Always there is that downward tug pulling us into animalistic inconsequence, into the mere seeking and fulfilling of immediate desires. Always there is that other tug (I don't want to call it upwards, because it really isn't) into abstraction, into removing ourselves from the physical reality of the here and now, from the call to embrace in love the concrete reality in which we are situated. A sort of pseudo-angelism that reduces our physical nature to a mere accident of being.

There is nothing new about these struggles. Technology simply happens to be the current arena in which they are being played out. Technology, because it is changing so quickly how we relate to one another and to the world we live in, promotes this pseudo-angelism of increasing abstraction, removal from the immediate environment. At the same time, by making floods of images and information so instantly available, it facilitates our descent to animalistic satiation and loss of transcendent meaning. It is not a new situation, just a very intense and marked expression of the same old struggle we've always had.

"So are you going to tell people what to do?" My superior, Fr. David May, asked me this as we walked back together from Mass the other day. He had just read the first seven chapters of the book, and was wondering if I would ever get around to making specific suggestions about how to navigate through all these murky technological waters.

"No, I don't think so," was my answer. For one thing, any specific suggestion I gave about Facebook, i-pads, i-pods or Twitter would be laughably outdated within a year of publication (an ethereal voice is heard from the year 2014: "Ha! Ha! He's still talking about 'friends' and 'tweets.' What a maroon!") (My ethereal voices always sound like Bugs Bunny, by the way.)

More importantly, though, is that the very struggle to stay human, to be human, to embrace the fullness of our humanity in a vital, vigorous, passionate way requires that we each plunge into the battle personally. To provide a list of helpful dos and don'ts, which would probably not be all that terribly helpful anyhow, reduces our humanity to a formula.

No, I won't do that, even if I could. What is needed today, urgently, is not so much a list of rules and don'ts, as a vision of humanity. What does it mean to be human? What does it look like? What good is it, anyhow, and is there any point in struggling to preserve it?

This is precisely what I have tried to offer in this book. The human being plunged into this world in all its physical earthy reality yet with a mind and soul open to heaven and to God, called to journey through the world fully engaged with every bit of it while striving to love every bit of it as does the God in whose image we are made. And these human beings are called to a communion of love in which every relationship with every other person is based on profound reverence and respect for their own mystery and beauty; this is the vision of human life that we must contemplate, preserve, and seek to live out.

And so the world of modern information technology, with its tendency to reduce human presence to on-screen pseudonymous avatars, to facilitate narcissism and solipsism, to diffuse our attention with trivia, gossip, and chat, to remove us from real and full presence to the incarnate world in which we are situated; this world of modern information technology has to be, not rejected (which is impossible in our current position), but *humanized*.

What we are and what we struggle to become as fully alive human beings is far more vital, more crucial, more essential to the world's happiness and prospering than all of the flashing lights, bells and whistles, power-ups and ever-increasing functionalities which the architects of the digital world continue to offer us.

If we lose our humanity, if we allow ourselves to be reduced to the confines and paradigms, the protocols and profiles of the digital world, then we have nothing to offer either it or the real world in which it is situated. It is analogous to the old joke about "200 TV channels, and nothing on." We could end up with seven billion "channels," the whole human race living in some vast on-line community, with no one having anything to say.

Without that silence in which we become a person, without those vital real

relationships that plunge us into the passion of love, without the innate dignity that a proper sense of privacy gives us, and without living our humanity freely and thoughtfully, fully immersed in the real world God made — without all of that, which I have tried in this book to show that technology imperils today, we will have nothing to say.

We will be barbarians. Barbarians with e-mail accounts, Twitter feeds, and i-pads, but barbarians nonetheless. We will be dummies with smart phones, twits who tweet, using Kindles but with no inner flame of our own, on Facebook but with no faces to speak of, nothing to present to the world but tired re-hashes of clichés and catchphrases.

We can do better than that. We *are* better than that. And we have to do better than that. We owe it to ourselves, to the rest of the world, to our children especially.

So what do we need to do? Well, we probably do have to make conscious choices about just how much we are going to be immersed in the digital world. Its tendencies, what it does to us, the ways it shapes us and our behaviors are, I hope, clear enough at this point. If we do not want that kind of technologically delimited humanity to be our whole humanity, we have to do something about it. Simply put, we just have to walk away from the machines from time to time. How much, how little, what each person can or should do in those terms: sorry, but you're on your own there!

What do you need from the technology? What good is it bringing you? What's it doing to you? What is the cost of your spending "x" time on the Internet or whatever? What are the other factors in your life that help you to broaden your humanity out from the limited and limiting presence of your technological devices? All these questions have to be considered as all human beings make the I-choice they must make.

And it all must be considered and navigated in light of our deepest beliefs, our deepest sense of purpose and meaning. What's it all about, and how are we to respond to what it's all about? We have to live deeply, think seriously, be alert in our minds, our spirits, and our senses to the most essential questions of life.

You may have different answers, different fundamental beliefs than I do. But we must all act in a way consistent with our most fundamental and seriously considered beliefs. Then, we will know what to do about Facebook and Twitter and i-pods. Then, we will know what we need to do.

Discernment of spirits: that's what it's all about. The one thing we cannot do, what we have never been able to do as human beings, is to just drift along on the current of life.

No, never, not for a moment! We have to fight, to work, to live, to move purposefully with a total engagement of our intellects and wills. That is what keeps us human, and that is the choice you and I and all of us together must make as we live and move and have our being in this digital age.